SINGAPORE
Trade, Investment and Economic Performance

SINGAP★RE
Trade, Investment and Economic Performance

Ramkishen S Rajan
George Mason University, USA

Shandre M Thangavelu
National University of Singapore, Singapore

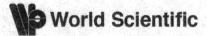 **World Scientific**

EW JERSEY · LONDON · SINGAPORE · BEIJING · SHANGHAI · HONG KONG · TAIPEI · CHENNAI

Published by

World Scientific Publishing Co. Pte. Ltd.

5 Toh Tuck Link, Singapore 596224

USA office: 27 Warren Street, Suite 401-402, Hackensack, NJ 07601

UK office: 57 Shelton Street, Covent Garden, London WC2H 9HE

British Library Cataloguing-in-Publication Data
A catalogue record for this book is available from the British Library.

SINGAPORE
Trade, Investment and Economic Performance

ISBN-13 978-981-4273-13-8
ISBN-10 981-4273-13-9

Typeset by Stallion Press
Email: enquiries@stallionpress.com

Printed in Singapore.

Contents

Chapter 1

Introduction: Economic Structure and External Orientation

The rapid evolution of Singapore from a modest trading post under colonial rule into a modern, prosperous, self-confident and sovereign nation is one of the more notable success growth and development stories of the second half of the 20th century. The Singapore economy has experienced one of the highest rates of growth in the world over the past three decades, its Gross Domestic Product (GDP) rising at an annual average rate of about 7.6% during the period 1970–2005. The growth has in turn propelled Singapore's average real per capita income from US\$ 512 in 1965 to its current level of over US\$ 26,982 by 2005, which is one of the highest in the world, surpassing many developed countries (Figure 1).

However, long-term averages hide the fact that the Singapore economy has been fairly fragile over the last five years. Specifically, following the sharp downturn in the global electronics industry and the sluggish regional and global growth, Singapore experienced an acute economic contraction in 2001; the recession was the worst in thirty years. Its impact on rising rates of redundancies, bankruptcies, financial and asset markets, consumer and business sentiment, and the like, have been deep and wide-spread. The depth of the recession was largely due to the confluence of a number of negative factors, including the unfortunate and horrendous events of September 11, 2001, Bird flu and SARS, Tsunami, Middle-East war, oil-shocks and

1

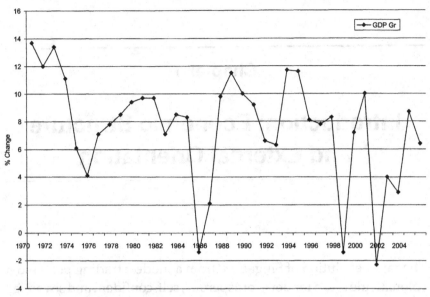

Source: Singapore Department of Statistics.

Fig. 1. GDP Growth for Singapore Economy: 1970–2005 (2000 Market Prices).

dot.com bubble crash, and it emphasized once again the acute susceptibility of the city state to external shocks. Indeed, the Singapore economy has appeared relatively fragile and much more at risk to boom-bust cycles post Asian crisis.[1] It is only in the last few years that the economy has regained its robustness. The Singapore economy expanded at a strong pace of 8.7% and 6.4% in 2004 and 2005, respectively, with the growth momentum being sustained in 2006–2007.

---

[1]Singapore was one of the few economies in East Asia to have staved off outright contraction that year despite the city state's intensive trade and financial linkages with the other crisis-hit economies. This admirable performance was due to a combination of strong fundamentals of the economy and prompt devaluation of the Singapore dollar (unlike the rigidity of the Hong Kong dollar, for instance). Somewhat less certain was the impact of the set of cost measures including a 10% reduction in the employers' contribution to the Central Provident Fund (a mandatory pension fund, voluntary wage reductions), cuts in nominal wages, government-controlled rentals for commercial and industrial properties and utility charges for electricity and telecommunications (Rajan *et al.*, 2002).

Table 1. Key Macroeconomic Indicators, 1999–2005

	1999	2000	2001	2002	2003	2004	2005
Real GDP (2000 market price & % change)	7.2	10.0	−2.3	4.0	2.9	8.7	6.4
Manufacturing	13.6	15.3	−12.8	8.4	3.0	13.9	9.3
Services	6.0	9.0	1.9	4.0	3.3	7.6	6.0
Construction	−8.8	−1.7	−1.2	−14.0	−9.0	−6.1	−1.1
Share of Gross Value Added (%)							
Manufacturing	23.1	26.8	23.7	25.8	26.3	27.7	27.3
Services	63.6	61.9	64.5	63.5	63.4	63.0	63.8
Construction	7.9	6.3	6.1	5.4	5.0	4.3	3.7
Others	5.1	5.0	5.7	5.3	5.3	5.0	5.2
Employment Share (%)							
Manufacturing	21.0	20.8	18.8	18.2	17.9	17.3	21.4
Services	71.1	65.5	74.2	75.0	75.6	76.3	69.6
Construction	6.9	13.1	6.1	5.9	5.6	5.5	8.1
Others	1.0	0.6	0.9	0.9	0.9	0.9	0.9
Unemployment rate (average)	3.5	3.1	3.3	3.6	4.0	3.4	3.2

Services sector includes: Wholesale and retail trade, hotels and restaurants, transport and communication, financial services, business services, other services. *Source*: Thangavelu and Toh (2005).

1.1. Sectoral Growth

At a sectoral level, while the construction sector has remained a drag on the economy, the economic rebound in recent years has largely been due to both non-construction manufacturing and services sectors. The manufacturing sector grew at an average pace of 8.5% between 2002 and 2005, while the services output growth averaged 5%. Within services, the wholesale & retail trade has been growing and double digits. The hotels and restaurants, financial services and transport and communications have also all rebounded in the last few years, hence driving services sector growth (Table 2). The service sector has consistently accounted for over 60% of Singapore's gross value-added, while the manufacturing sector has accounted for about 25%. There is a conscious policy by the government to ensure that both the manufacturing and services continue to form the "twin engines" of growth for the economy.

Table 2. Key Economic Indicators by Sectors (2000 Market Prices — Change in %)

	2002	2003	2004	2005
Total	4.0	2.9	8.7	6.4
Goods Producing Industries	3.9	1.1	10.5	7.7
Manufacturing	8.4	3.0	13.9	9.3
Construction	−14.0	−9.0	−6.1	−1.1
Services Producing Industries	4.0	3.3	7.6	6.0
Wholesale & Retail Trade	8.2	10.6	15.6	10.5
Hotels & Restaurants	−2.4	−8.7	11.5	4.6
Transport & Communications	6.3	−0.7	8.5	4.5
Financial Services	−3.4	7.6	5.4	6.5
Business Services	3.9	−1.0	2.8	4.9

Source: Singapore Department of Statistics.

1.2. Employment and Income Distribution

As would be expected, employment growth has lagged economic recovery and unemployment peaked at 4% in 2003. However, the strong output growth since then has been complemented by robust employment growth in 2004 and 2005 (Table 3). The overall unemployment rate has consequently declined to 3.1% in 2005. Notwithstanding this decline in cyclical unemployment, the structural adjustment of the economy to higher value-added activities appears to have contributed to the slower trend growth in employment and a consequent rise in the number of structural unemployed Singapore residents (Figure 2). The economy also relies heavily on foreign workers to augment its labor force as well as to plug gaps in human capital requirements of industry (Figure 3).

Table 3. Labor Market, 2002–2005

	2002	2003	2004	2005
Labor Force ('000) (As at June)	2,321	2,312	2,342	2,367
Employed Persons ('000) (As at Year-End)	2,148	2,135	2,207	2,320
Unemployment Rate (%) (Average)	3.6	4.0	3.4	3.1
Changes in Employment (Number)	−22,900	−12,900	71,400	113,300

Sources: Singapore Department of Statistics; Ministry of Manpower.

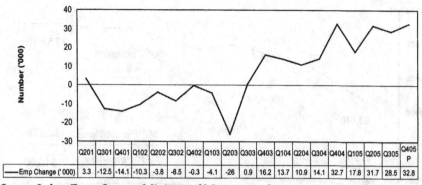

	Q201	Q301	Q401	Q102	Q202	Q302	Q402	Q103	Q203	Q303	Q403	Q104	Q204	Q304	Q404	Q105	Q205	Q305	Q405 P
—Emp Change ('000)	3.3	-12.5	-14.1	-10.3	-3.8	-8.5	-0.3	-4.1	-26	0.9	16.2	13.7	10.9	14.1	32.7	17.8	31.7	28.5	32.8

Source: Labor Force Survey, Ministry of Manpower, Singapore.

Fig. 2. The Long-Term Unemployment in Singapore (%), 2001–2005.

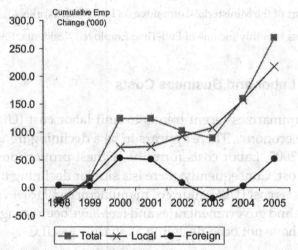

Source: Ministry of Manpower, Singapore.

Fig. 3. Cumulative Employment Change for Singapore Economy by Local and Foreign Workers, 1988–2005.

The structural changes in the economy have also created new challenges in terms of widening income gap in the economy. The income of lower 20th percentile appears to have stagnated while that of the top 10th percentile has risen markedly. As with many other countries that have embraced the forces of globalization, this widening income gap presents some important challenges that need to be addressed by policymakers (Figure 4).

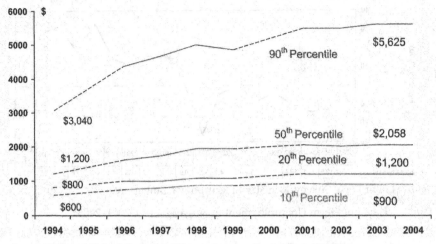

Source: Report of the Ministerial Committee on Low Wage Workers.

Fig. 4.   Gross Monthly Income of Full-Time Employed Residents, 1994–2004.

1.3. Unit Labor and Business Costs

Table 4 summarizes recent trends in unit labor cost (ULC) for the Singapore economy. There appears to be a declining trend between 2002 and 2005. Labor costs form the highest proportion of overall business cost. Consequently, there is a similar declining trend in the unit business cost (UBC) index of manufacturing. However, the cost of services and government rates and fees have been rising, implying the UBCs have not been declining as sharply as ULCs.

Table 4. Indices of Unit Labor and Unit Business Costs for Singapore Economy (2000 base year)

	2002	2003	2004	2005
Unit Labor Cost Index of Overall Economy	102.6	100.8	96.9	95.4
Unit Business Cost Index of Manufacturing	102.5	100.9	97.9	97.7
— Unit Labor Cost	106.6	102.5	95.0	92.2
— Services Cost	99.4	99.9	100.4	102.4
— Government Rates & Fees	89.4	86.5	95.1	96.2

Source: Singapore Department of Statistics.

1.4. Development Strategies

While the openness of the Singapore economy makes it imperative that that ULCs are kept at a competitive level, in the new global economy, comparative advantage is based increasingly on knowledge and creativity than on traditional factor inputs. Entrepreneurship is the conduit between investments in knowledge and economic growth (Audretsch, 2003). There is in fact a fairly new and growing body of econometric evidence which suggests that entrepreneurship is a key determinant of economic growth in a knowledge-based economy. The Singapore government has long recognized the importance of nurturing local entrepreneurship. For instance, the city state's Minister for Manpower, Lee Boon Yang, has noted:

> Value-creation through creativity, innovation and entrepreneurship Second, the new economy is driven by innovation and value-creation. To prosper, we have to become a high value-added knowledge-based economy. To succeed in this environment, you must be creative and entrepreneurial. The ability to generate new ideas, and bring them to market before your competitors, is very important. Singaporeans are disciplined and productive workers. They said we are good at execution but lacking in creative thinking. We must be bolder and more innovative in order to succeed. We must also be more entrepreneurial so as to transform ideas into value. Every good idea has to be developed into marketable goods and services. We need more Singaporeans who are prepared for the risk and rewards of bringing ideas to the market (Lee, 2002).

Accordingly, the Singapore government has forged a commitment to create an environment conducive for entrepreneurial activity and fostering a culture of learning and experimentation. In this regard, it has offered a number of targeted incentives to promote it, especially in the area of high technology (i.e. so-called "technopreneurship").[2]

While developing local entrepreneurship is of importance, there is also a need to maximize benefits from foreign investments (Chia, 1992). Foreign multinational corporations (MNCs) bring with them

---

[2]Ho *et al.* (2002) attempt to define the term "technopreneurship" and discuss steps to facilitate its growth in Singapore.

state of the art technology and access to global networks. Greater attention has been placed on strengthening the base of small and medium local enterprises (SMEs) and create and strengthen strategic partnerships and skill linkages between SMEs and MNCs by promoting local sourcing, sub-contracting and technological and R&D spillovers and capabilities (also see Hu and Shin, 2002).

Since the late 1980s, and especially the 1990s, the Singapore government has undertaken an aggressive strategy of building up its external wing by investing heavily in regional and extra regional trading partners (Yeung, 2000). The government remains committed to developing a breed of world-class companies which have a global reach. The government-linked companies (GLCs) are viewed as the "primary instruments through which the state inaugurates the regionalization drive" (Yeung, 2000, p. 21). The *Business Times* of Singapore (July 2002) makes the following observation about GLCs:

> The Singapore GLC, or government-linked company, was a necessary Singapore invention. At a time when the local economy was a fledgling, this breed of corporation helped it to take flight. Since the time Temasek (Holdings) was formed in 1974 as the government's investment holding arm, it has grown to include 65 major companies, with a myriad of subsidiaries and associate companies in almost every economic sector, with a workforce totaling 150,000. The top 22 GLCs accounted for 13% of the country's gross domestic product in 1998. The top seven listed GLCs had a market capitalization of $72 billion as at end-May, or 21% of the Singapore Exchange's total capitalization.

The government, through Temasek Holdings, has significant equity in many of Singapore's largest companies in vast areas of the economy including port and marine, shipping and logistics, banking & financial services, real estate, airline, telecommunications and media, power and utilities.[3]

While acknowledging the world-class technocratic capabilities of the Singapore government, Bhaskaran (2003) suggests that the state's role in Singapore might have become more of a liability and needs to be rolled back in certain areas. In particular, he argues that the government intervention in terms of its ownership and management of

---

[3]See www.temasekholdings.com.sg/.

the majority of land and other critical resources has distorted relative prices, while the domination of GLCs in local economic activity has curbed private sector initiative by pre-empting local business opportunities. In similar vein, the IMF (2000) makes the following observation:

> Although the GLCs have been expected to operate on a competitive basis in both domestic and international markets (and indeed most of them have remained profitable, generating large operating surpluses), their overwhelming market power is likely to have crowded out local private enterprises and thus prevented the development of a large and dynamic network of local corporations, contributing to the widely perceived lack of corporate dynamism in Singapore (p. 11).

The Singapore government is clearly cognisant of these assessments. They have recognized that while there was a need for strong role of the state in the early stages of growth to address market failures in the economy, the role of the state in economic development must undergo a transformation as the economy develops and becomes more sophisticated. Accordingly, the government is reducing its direct role in the economy by gradually divesting its stake in GLCs and allowing greater competition in the services sector in particular (Economic Review Committee, 2003; WTO, 2004).

1.5. Free Trade Agreements (FTAs)

The cornerstone of Singapore's economic strategy has been its openness to international trade and investment flows. Advances in the Information systems, Communications and related Technologies (ICT) have significantly shrunk economic distances between nations and markets and is possibly reducing the demand for some conventional roles such as entrepot, overseas headquarters (OHQs) and other hub services and ancillary services. This, along with the fact that Singapore is probably the most open economy in the world (with a trade to GDP ratio of about 250%) with few natural resources, implies the need for the city-state to be particularly aware of and responsive to the powerful forces that are transforming markets and dramatically changing ways of doing business, so as to remain "ahead of the game". This is especially so as the competition for investments, export markets and skilled labor intensifies as more economies embrace open door trade and investment policies and some of Singapore's hub roles are duplicated by lower cost regional rivals.

In an effort to ensure sustained growth of Singapore's exports, the city state has attempted to aggressively source preferential trade accords ("free trade agreements" or FTAs in common parlance) with a number of countries in Asia and elsewhere. FTAs are not an entirely new component of Singapore's commercial trade strategy which in turn is the cornerstone of the city state's larger international economic policy. While being among the most ardent of supporters of the global trading system, Singapore has actively pursued a second track to liberalization via the regional route in the 1980s and 1990s. Regionalism has hitherto involved both the Southeast Asian region via the ten-member ASEAN (Association of Southeast Asian Nations) grouping and the larger Asia and Pacific region via the twenty-one member APEC (Asia Pacific Economic Cooperation) grouping. However, indications are that the regional financial crisis 1997–1998 has held up the pace if not commitment by some of the ASEAN members to trade liberalization, while APEC has become rather unwieldy and appears ill-equipped to handle substantive trade and investment liberalization issues effectively. Accordingly, Singapore policy makers have underscored the need to explore alternative liberalization paths, i.e. a third track. Sourcing of trade pacts on a bilateral basis — bilateralism for short — has become an integral part of Singapore's new commercial trade strategy (Rajan and Sen, 2002; Thangavelu and Toh, 2005).

As of November 2006, apart from the ASEAN Free Trade Agreement (AFTA), Singapore has signed trade agreements with Australia, European Free Trade Association (EFTA), Jordan, India, Japan, Korea, New Zealand, Panama, Trans-Pacific SEP (Brunei, New Zealand, Chile, Singapore), United States of America (USA). Singapore is also negotiating bilateral agreements with Bahrain, Canada, China, Egypt, Mexico, Pakistan, Peru, Sri Lanka, Kuwait, Qatar and the United Arab Emirates (UAE). On a regional basis, Singapore through ASEAN is negotiating agreements with ASEAN's full-dialogue partners, viz. China, Australia and New Zealand, India, Japan and Korea.

Singapore's choice of partners as part of its trade strategy of bilateralism may be broadly divided into two groups. The first group, which includes the US and Japan, are major established trading partners, constituting some one third of the city state's total merchandise trade. These economic giants are also major investors in the city state as they are in Southeast Asia at large. Bilateral trade accords with these two economies are best seen as a formalization of the *de facto* extensive and deep linkages that already exist. Entering into broad-ranging trade agreements with them is not only a means by which Singapore might gain greater market access (with Japan in particular) but is also a way of avoiding the possible imposition of protectionist measures in the future (with regard to the US in particular), as well as managing future trade tensions, including establishing orderly dispute settlement mechanisms. Being among the first few countries to establish trade accords with these two and other economically significant economies also ensures that Singapore is not discriminated *ex-post* in the event that its "trade competitors" form such pacts with third countries. The second group of countries with which Singapore is attempting to formalize or has formalized trade accords, including India, Australia, New Zealand and the EFTA countries, individually do not account for more than 3% of either Singapore's total exports, domestic exports, or total imports. The aim here is to seek out new markets and sources of and opportunities for investment.

1.6. Structure of the Book

Chapter 2 offers a brief overview of Singapore's FDI regime and FDI patterns. Chapter 3 addresses the emerging trade patterns of the Singapore economy and outlines relevant trade policies. Chapter 4 discusses recent initiatives undertaken by the city-state pertaining to trade and investment related infrastructure. Chapter 5 considers Singapore's trade policies and issues relating to the services sector focussing on the city state's multilateral and bilateral commitments. As will be apparent, deepening economic relations with India has dominated the story of Singapore's growing economic engagement with South Asia. Accordingly, Chapter 6 considers the specific case of Singapore's bilateral economic relations with India which have been blossoming in recent times and is a good case-study of intensifying East and South Asia economic linkages in general. Chapter 7 highlights some policy challenges and implications for the Singapore economy going forward.

Chapter 2

Foreign Direct Investment (FDI): Policies, Trends and Patterns

2.1. FDI Regime

The Singapore government has a conscious policy of actively encouraging FDI inflows. The Economic Development Board (EDB) was established in 1961 as a one-stop agency to lead Singapore's industrialization drive through encouraging export-oriented FDI into Singapore. To this end the EDB has worked very closely with various ministries and other government bodies to facilitate FDI. While the initial emphasis of the EDB was on labor intensive manufacturing, over the years the focus has shifted to encouraging inflows in higher value-added areas and skill-intensive manufacturing activities as well as knowledge-based professional services service sector activities such as financial services, ICT services and offshore services. Businesses are also encouraged to establish Research and Development (R&D) facilities in the city state as well as use the country as an international or regional headquarters. The emphasis of Singapore's FDI promotion has always been on developing clusters. Thus, the EDB helped develop chemical, electronics and engineering clusters, all of which became key economic engines for Singapore. More recently emphasis has been on product development, biomedical research, educational and health care services.[4]

---

[4]See Chia (2005) and Lall (2000) for discussions of Singapore's industrial policy.

Singapore does not impose any restrictions on foreign ownership in the manufacturing activities, but does maintain restrictions on key strategic sectors such as in national security reasons (arms and ammunition) and certain services sector. However, since the late 1990s, the government has been liberalizing the services sector by relaxing foreign ownership in key services industries. For instance, in financial services, the 40% limit on foreign ownership of local banks was lifted in 1999. The 70% limit on foreign ownership was removed in the Stock Exchange of Singapore (SES) and foreign ownership restrictions were completely removed in telecommunication services in 2002. However, the government still maintains ownership restrictions in specific professional services such as in air transport, law, and media (newspaper publishing). Overall, the Singapore government neither screens FDI inflows nor does it maintain policies on performance requirements, and it has fairly liberal investment regulations. Singapore largely complies with WTO Trade-Related Investment Measures (TRIMS) obligations. Singapore has signed Investment Guarantee Agreements (IGAs) with its ASEAN members and a number of other countries. These agreements offer mutual protection of nationals or companies of either country against war and non-commercial risks of expropriation and nationalization. In addition the city state has signed a number of trade pacts, most of which offer some for of investor protection. In any event, the Singapore government has not expropriated foreign investments in the past.

Singapore was ranked as the third easiest economy in which to do business, after New Zealand and the United States (World Bank, 2005). The government provides world-class infrastructure for foreign investments, but also believes in providing competitive direct and indirect incentives for multinational activities in key sectors. The incentives normally include concessionary corporate tax rates of between 5% to 15% or corporate income tax exemptions. The government is also offering incentives in R&D activities and intellectual property rights (IPRs), and tax concessions on royalties. Table 1 summarizes some of the regulations of and incentives for FDI

Table 1. Summary of Main Incentives to Attract Foreign Investments

Scheme	Eligibility	Incentives
Approved Foreign Loan Scheme	Minimum loan of S$200,000 from a foreign lender to purchase of productive equipment.	Complete or partial exemption from withholding tax on interest payable to the lender.
Approved Royalties Incentive	Payment of royalties to a foreign partner.	Complete or partial exemption from withholding tax on royalties.
Development and Expansion Incentive	Companies undertaking new projects or expanding existing projects that provide significant economic gains to Singapore.	Concessional tax rate of 5% to 15% for qualifying income streams.
Double deduction for R&D expenditure	Manufacturing and services firms engaged in R&D.	Double deduction for qualifying R&D expenses against income.
Investment Allowance Incentive	Proposed investment to be made within a qualifying period of not more than five years.	Exemption on a specified proportion of expenditure of new fixed investment in productive investment.
International Headquarters	Companies providing management and other approved headquarters-related services to subsidiary, associated companies in other countries.	Concessional tax rate on income from providing qualifying HQ services to approved network companies.
Pioneer Status	New manufacturing and service investments introducing skills substantially more advanced than the average industry level.	Exemption from corporate income tax on qualifying profits for up to ten years.
Regional Headquarters	Companies providing management and other approved headquarters-related services to subsidiary, associated companies on a regional scale.	Concessional tax rate of 15% on income from providing qualifying HQ services to approved companies for three years.

(Continued)

Table 1. (*Continued*)

Scheme	Eligibility	Incentives
R&D and IP management hub scheme	Companies engaged in R&D and/or intellectual property management activities from Singapore.	Exemption for a period of 5 financial years on foreign-sourced royalties or foreign-sourced interest remitted to Singapore to be spent on R&D.
Tax Concessions on royalty income from approved inventions and innovations	Royalty income arising from an approved invention or approved innovations.	Royalty income will be taxed (at 10%) on 10% of gross royalty or net royalty income (after deductions), whichever is lower.
Technopreneur investment incentive	Companies that invest in qualifying Singapore based technopreneurial start-up activity.	An investor in an approved company can deduct losses incurred from selling shares in the approved company against his own taxable income.
Venture capital fund incentive	Venture funds with activities in Singapore.	Complete or partial corporate tax exemption, for a set period, on income from divestment of shares, foreign dividend and foreign interest income.
Writing-down allowance for acquisition of know-how	Companies engaged in Intellectual Property management activities in Singapore.	Allows amortization of acquisition costs over five years for tax purpose.
Writing-down allowance for cost sharing agreement	Companies that have signed cost-sharing agreement to cost-sharing the expenses on R&D.	Allows amortization over one to five years of cost sharing payments to R&D, which could otherwise not to be deductible.

Source: Economic Development Board, Singapore.

in Singapore.[5] A more comprehensive list of investment regulations and incentives is provided in Annex 1.

2.2. Trends and Patterns of FDI to and from Singapore

Table 2 outlines the sources of Singapore's FDI between 1997 and 2003 by country. With regard to FDI inflows, as is apparent, the United States, EU, and Japan are the key countries sources of investment. FDI from Europe has increased strongly from 35% in 1997–1999 to nearly 40% in 2000–2003. The US share has remained fairy stable at 15–16%, while Japan's share has declined from 17% to less than 14%. Table 3 provides the sources of FDI inflows to Singapore by region. Interestingly, Europe has overtaken Asia as the largest group of investors, accounting for 45% of total FDI in 2004, up from 29% in 1995. North America's share (US and Canada) has declined slightly from 20% to 17%. Within Europe, the Netherlands, Switzerland and the United Kingdom (UK) constitute the bulk of

Table 2. Direction of FDI Inflows into Singapore (%), 1997–2003

	1997–1999	2000–2003
United States	15.0	16.6
Europe	35.5	40.0
— Netherlands	10.0	13.5
— Switzerland	9.0	7.2
— UK	9.2	8.8
Malaysia	4.0	2.7
Japan	17.0	13.8
Australia	2.2	1.3
Latin America	14.6	16.3
Others	11.7	9.3

Source: Singapore Statistical Yearbook, Department of Statistics, Singapore.

---

[5]Also see Chia (2005). For a critical evaluation of the use of investment incentives, see Rajan (2004) and references cited within.

Table 3. Sources of FDI Inflows in Singapore by Regions, 1995, 2000 and 2004

	1995	2000	2004
Europe	29%	38%	45%
Asia	34%	24%	21%
US & Canada	20%	19%	17%
Australia and New Zealand	4%	2%	1%
Others	13%	17%	16%

Source: Foreign Equity Investment in Singapore, various issues, Department of Statistics, Singapore.

FDI inflows to Singapore. Investments from Australia and New Zealand have declined in relative terms from 4% in 1995 to 1% in 2004. Interestingly, "others", which include countries from the Middle East, has grown from 13% in 1995 to around 16–17%.

It is noteworthy that Asia's share has slumped from 34% in 1995 to 21% by 2004. While this is largely a reflection of the decline in Japan's FDI share as noted above, it would be useful to examine the breakdown of FDI inflows to Singapore from Asia (Table 4).

Table 4. Source of Asia's FDI Inflows in Singapore by Country, 1995, 2000 and 2004

	1995	2000	2004
Brunei Darussalam	0.7%	0.5%	0.5%
Indonesia	2.8%	3.7%	2.9%
Malaysia	12.4%	10.9%	8.1%
Philippines	1.3%	2.3%	1.6%
Thailand	2.8%	1.5%	1.7%
Vietnam	0.0%	0.0%	0.0%
China	1.2%	2.0%	0.4%
Hong Kong	13.8%	12.7%	7.9%
Japan	59.8%	55.7%	58.2%
South Korea	0.8%	2.2%	2.5%
Taiwan	3.3%	7.5%	10.5%
Other Asia	1.2%	1.0%	5.7%

Source: Foreign Equity Investment in Singapore, various issues, Department of Statistics, Singapore.

Interestingly Japan's share of Asia's FDI into Singapore has remained fairly stable since 1995 at around 60%. The other two traditional Asian investors in Singapore are Malaysia and Hong Kong. Both these economies were responsible for 25% of Asian FDI flows to Singapore in 1995 but their shares declined to 16% in 2004. In contrast, FDI from Taiwan has risen from 3.3% of overall Asian FDI flows to Singapore in 1995 to 10.5% by 2004. Thus, Taiwan has overtaken Hong Kong and Malaysia as sources of FDI inflows. Indonesia, South Korea, Thailand and Philippines follow as the next largest investors in 2004, each contributing 2–3% of total FDI to Singapore. Anecdotal evidence suggests that Indian firms have begun to establish headquarters in Singapore as a platform to East Asia. This is reflected in the rising share of "Other Asia" from 1.2% in 1995 to 5.7% by 2004 (see Section 6 for a detailed elaboration on Singapore–India ties).

Table 5 breaks down FDI into Singapore by industry. Around 35% of FDI inflows to Singapore have gone to the manufacturing sector and the rest into the services sector. Within services, the financial & insurance and commerce and business services account for the bulk of FDI inflows.

As noted, since the early 1990s, Singapore has also been heavily investing both in the region as well as globally as a means of expanding its external wing a policy that has been led by Singapore's major government holding company (Temasek) and

Table 5. FDI Inflow to Singapore by Industry (%), 1998–2003

	1997–1999	2000–2003
Manufacturing	34.0	36.0
Commerce	15.2	14.8
Transport & Communication	3.7	4.5
Financial & Insurance	36.6	37.0
Real Estate	3.4	3.0
Business Services	3.6	4.1
Others	3.5	0.6

Source: Singapore Statistical Yearbook, Department of Statistics, Singapore.

Table 6. Direction of FDI Inflows from Singapore (%), 1997–2003

	1997–1999	2000–2003
United States	5.4	5.8
Europe	13.3	9.4
— Netherlands	2.5	1.0
— Switzerland	0.5	0.3
— UK	3.9	4.9
Malaysia	9.4	8.3
Japan	1.3	2.4
Australia	2.5	2.4
Latin America	13.3	24.7
China	15.5	13.2
Hong Kong	10.5	8.2
Thailand	3.5	3.0
Chinese Taipei	2.9	2.4
Korea	2.0	1.8
India	0.6	1.1
Others	19.8	16.6

Source: Singapore Statistical Yearbook, Department of Statistics, Singapore.

other government linked companies (GLCs) and facilitated by various government agencies including International Enterprise Singapore (IE Singapore), Economic Development Board (EDB) and the Standards, Productivity and Innovation Board (SPRING). What have been the main destinations of Singapore's FDI?

As is apparent from Table 6, Singapore's FDI outflows have been distributed across the world. The share of FDI to the US has remained stable at around 5%. Europe has been the key destination, accounting for 13% of Singapore's outflows between 1997 and 1999 and just over 9% between 2000 and 2003. Singapore has also invested aggressively in Malaysia and Hong Kong, both of which made up 20% of the city-state's outward investments in 1997–1999 and 16% in 2000–2003. China has also been an important destination for Singapore investments (15% in 1997–1999 and 13% in 2000–2003). Beyond Asia, Europe and the US, one-third of Singapore's investments went to Latin America, Middle East

Table 7. FDI Outflows from Singapore by Industry (%), 1998–2003

	1997–1999	2000–2003
Manufacturing	24.9	20.2
Commerce	8.2	7.0
Transport & Communication	6.0	8.0
Financial & Insurance	48.2	55.0
Real Estate	7.4	5.2
Business Services	2.7	1.2
Others	2.6	3.4

Source: Singapore Statistical Yearbook, Department of Statistics, Singapore.

and other areas in 1997–1999, with this share increasing to two-fifth in 2000–2003. This suggests that Singapore's investments have been fairly well diversified and are becoming more so over the years, though on a stock basis Asia still dominates (UNCTAD, 2005).

Table 7 reveals the sectoral shares of FDI outflows from Singapore. Half of Singapore's outward investments have been related to finance and insurance, a reflection of aggressive outward orientation of Singapore's financial institutions since the late 1990s. This sector appears to be gaining in importance as countries in the region and elsewhere continue to liberalize their financial sectors. About 20% of investments from Singapore have been to the manufacturing sector though the share has declined from 25% in 1997–1999 to 20% in 2000–2003.

Singapore companies also invest overseas in the commerce and real estate areas. Table 8 summarizes the top 15 cross-border mergers and acquisitions (M&As) by Singapore companies between 1997 and 2004. Apart from two purchases in Hong Kong (Dao Heng Bank and DBS Diamond Holdings) and Indonesia (Indostat and Telkomsel), the rest are in North America, Australia and Europe. Of the top 15 M&A purchases between 1997 and 2004 most were in electrical and electronics, transportation and finance, area of competitiveness of Singaporean companies.

Table 8. Singapore's Top 15 Cross-border M&A Purchases, 1997–2004 (Millions of dollars)

Rank	Target company	Target industry	Target economy	Acquiring company	Acq ind	Value	Year
1	Cable & Wireless Optus Lt (C&W)	Telephone communications	Australia	SingTel (Singapore)	Radiotelephone communications	8,491.12	2001
2	Dao Heng Bank Group (Guoco)	Banks, non-US chartered	Hong Kong (China)	DBS Group Holdings Ltd	Banks, non-US chartered	5,679.70	2001
3	TXU Australia Ltd	Electric services	Australia	Singapore Power Pte Ltd	Electric services	3,720.00	2004
4	DII Group	Electronic components, nec	United States	Flextronics International Ltd	Printed circuit boards	2,591.00	2000
5	DBS Diamond Holdings Ltd	Investors, nec	Hong Kong (China)	DBS Bank	Banks, non-US chartered	1,964.93	2003
6	US Premium Office Properties	Operators of non-residential buildings	United States	Investor Group	Investors, nec	1,852.00	2004
7	ChipPAC Inc	Semiconductors and related devices	United States	ST Assembly Test Services Ltd	Instruments to measure electricity	1,458.68	2004
8	GPU PowerNet Pty Ltd	Combination utilities, nec	Australia	Singapore Power Pte Ltd	Electric services	1,264.00	2000
9	Virgin Atlantic Airways Ltd	Air transportation, scheduled	United Kingdom	Singapore Airlines Ltd	Air transportation, scheduled	884.00	2000

(Continued)

Table 8. (*Continued*)

Rank	Target company	Target industry	Target economy	Acquiring company	Acq ind	Value	Year
10	APL Ltd	Deep sea foreign transportation of freight	United States	Neptune Orient Lines Ltd	Transportation	878.50	1997
11	Gotaas-Larsen Shipping Corp	Deep sea foreign transportation of freight	Monaco	Osprey Maritime Ltd	Transportation	749.90	1997
12	Nortel-Mnfg Facilities (5)	Communications equipment, nec	Canada	Flextronics International Ltd	Printed circuit boards	725.00	2004
13	Indosat	Telephone communications	Indonesia	Singapore Technologies Telemed	Communications services, nec	635.06	2002
14	Telkomsel	Telephone communications	Indonesia	SingTel (Singapore)	Radiotelephone communications	627.00	2001
15	Hessenatie	Water transportation of freight, nec	Belgium	PSA Corp Ltd	Port services	605.48	2002

Source: UNCTAD (2005).

Chapter 3

Singapore's Trade Performance and Patterns with Emphasis on East and South Asia

3.1. Commodity Composition

Given Singapore's lack of natural resources, it is highly dependent on exports as well as imports for its growth (see Table 1). Since its independence in 1965, the Singapore economy relied heavily on the entrepot trade of goods, thereby building its trade networks globally. As seen from Table 1, re-exports have constituted at least 45% of total exports in recent times. In terms of total global merchandise trade, Singapore ranks among the top 20 major countries and accounts for nearly 2% of total global merchandise exports (US$ 230b) in 2005 (Table 2).

Figure 1 reveals that three-fifths of Singapore's total exports are concentrated in transport and machinery exports (SITC 7). However, the composition of exports in the SITC 7 has been changing since the Asian crisis. It appears from Table 3 that the share of exports of bio-medical and pharmaceutical products has increased over the years, rising from 6% in 1994 to 12% in 2005. Merchandise exports constitute around 60% of Singapore's total exports, with services making up the rest. This proportion has remained constant over the last few years. Within services transportation, travel and other services

Table 1. External Trade at Current Prices (Change in %)

	1979–1989	1999	2002	2005
Total	10.3	8.1	1.5	13.8
Imports	9.7	10.8	0.3	13.6
Exports	10.9	5.7	2.7	14.0
Domestic Exports	11.7	9.8	0.8	15.1
Oil	3.9	12.4	−3.9	41.5
Non-oil	16.4	9.5	10.6	8.2
Re-exports	9.6	0.2	8.0	12.7

Source: Economic Survey of Singapore, Ministry of Trade and Industry, various issues.

(including education) constitute about 35% of total service exports in 2005, down from 50% in 1994.

The share of imports of transport and machinery products (SITC 7) has been in the range of 50–60% of the city state's total imports (Figure 2). The import of intermediate goods indicates that the production structure in the economy is fragmented and integrated with the global production value-chain. The share of import of intermediate inputs (office machines & telecommunication equipments, non-electrical machinery, chemicals, etc.) constitutes more than 70% of its imports. Merchandise imports constitute around 70–75% of Singapore's total imports, with services making up the rest (Table 4). This proportion has remained constant in the last few years. Within services transportation, travel and other services (including education) have constituted about three-fifths of total service exports and this share has remained fairly stable.

3.2. Country Composition of Merchandise Trade[6]

Figure 3 reveals that the share of Asian merchandise exports from Singapore has been steadily increasing from around 50% in 1990 to

---

[6]Given the lack of data on services trade at a bilateral level, this section is inevitably limited to merchandise trade.

Table 2. Singapore's Position in Global Merchandise Trade, 2005

Rank	Exporters	Value (US $ billion)	Share in world total (%)	Rank	Importers	Value (US$ billion)	Share in world total (%)
1	Germany	969.9	9.3	1	United States	1732.4	16.1
2	United States	904.4	8.7	2	Germany	773.8	7.2
3	China	762.0	7.3	3	China	660.0	6.1
4	Japan	594.9	5.7	4	Japan	514.9	4.8
5	France	460.2	4.4	5	United Kingdom	510.2	4.7
6	Netherlands	402.4	3.9	6	France	497.9	4.6
7	United Kingdom	382.8	3.7	7	Italy	379.8	3.5
8	Italy	367.2	3.5	8	Netherlands	359.1	3.3
9	Canada	359.4	3.4	9	Canada	319.7	3.0
10	Belgium	334.3	3.2	10	Belgium	318.7	3.0
11	Hong Kong, China	292.1	2.8	11	Hong Kong, China	300.2	2.8
	domestic exports	20.1	0.2		retained imports[a]	28.1	0.3
	re-exports	272.1	2.6	12	Spain	278.8	2.6
12	Korea, Republic of	284.4	2.7	13	Korea, Republic of	261.2	2.4
13	Russian Federation	243.6	2.3	14	Mexico	231.7	2.1
14	**Singapore**	**229.6**	**2.2**	**15**	**Singapore**	**200.0**	**1.9**
	domestic exports	124.5	1.2		retained imports[a]	94.9	0.9
	re-exports	105.1	1.0	17	India	134.8	1.3
19	Malaysia	140.9	1.4	21	Australia[b]	125.3	1.2
25	Thailand	110.1	1.1	22	Thailand	118.2	1.1
27	Australia	105.8	1.0	24	Malaysia	114.6	1.1
29	India	95.1	0.9	31	Indonesia	69.5	0.6
31	Indonesia	86.2	0.8	40	Philippines	47.4	0.4
44	Philippines	41.3	0.4				
	World[c]	10,431.0	100.0		World[c]	10,783.0	100.0

Notes: [a] Retained imports are defined as imports less re-exports; [b] Imports are valued f.o.b.; [c] Includes significant re-exports or imports for re-export.
Source: International Trade Statistics 2006, WTO.

75% by 2005. The export shares for Singapore's key trading countries in Asia are given in Table 5. ASEAN is the main market for Singapore, absorbing nearly 25% of total exports from Singapore. However, ASEAN's export share has declined over the decade, from 30% in 1995. Within ASEAN, Malaysia is the dominant export destination. Before the Asian crisis, Malaysia absorbed nearly 19% of the total exports from Singapore. After the crisis, the export share to Malaysia has fallen to around 13% in 2005. The export share to Thailand also fell from almost 6% in 1995 to 4% in 2005. In contrast, the export shares of Indonesia increased from 2% in 1995

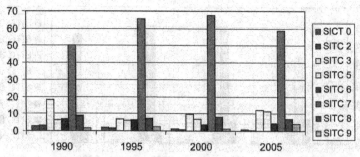

Source: Economic Survey of Singapore, Ministry of Trade and Industry, various issues.

Fig. 1. Singapore Total Export Composition (% of Total Export).

Table 3. Product Composition of Singapore's Exports (%), 1994–2005

	Exports			
	1994	1999	2003	2005
Electrical & Electronic Components and Machinery	45.6	55.3	50.8	58.8
Manufactured Goods	6.0	4.3	3.7	4.6
Chemicals & Pharmaceutical	5.7	8.0	11.8	11.4
Fuels and Petroleum Products	9.5	7.9	11.1	15.0
Textiles & Clothing	1.4	2.0	1.0	1.0
Transport Equipment	18.3	11.0	10.3	1.6
Food, Beverages, Crude Materials	4.4	3.3	1.9	2.2
Miscellaneous Manufactures	9.1	8.2	9.4	5.4
Export of Goods (values S$)	$145,079m	$196,004m	$281,699m	$386,919m
Export of Services (values S$)	$55,474m	$40,158m	$63,157m	$85,435m
Transportation	53.2	40.5	38.4	34.9
Travel	19.8	19.3	13.0	11.1
Financial & Insurance	0.7	5.9	8.7	9.4
Other Services	26.3	34.3	39.9	44.4

Sources: Ministry of Trade and Industry, Economic Survey of Singapore, various issues; *Yearbook of Statistics*, Singapore, various issues.

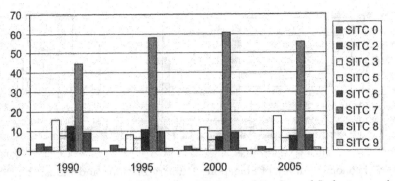

Source: Economic Survey of Singapore, Ministry of Trade and Industry, various issues.

Fig. 2.   Singapore Import Composition (% of total Imports).

to nearly 4% in 2005.[7] China and India are becoming important trading partners for Singapore as exports to both countries have been growing over 20% for the last two years (Figure 4). The share of exports to China increased from 2.3% in 1995 to nearly 8.6% in 2005. India's share of Singapore's exports increased from 1.6% in 1995 to nearly 2.6% in 2005. If current growth rates are sustained, India's share of Singapore's exports can be expected to rise more markedly the next few years (also see Section 6).

Table 5 highlights Singapore's export markets between 1991 and 2005. It is instructive to note that Asia's share of Singapore's exports have rose from 55% in 1991 to 68% by 2005. Table 6 highlights the share of Singapore's merchandise exports to various Asian economies. In 2005, exports of SITC 7 (Machine, Transport equipment) dominate Singapore's exports to most Asian economies except for Indonesia and Vietnam where SITC 3 (Mineral fuels) dominate. Singapore also export SITC 5 (viz. Chemical products) to the rest if Asia.

Figure 5 reveals that the share of Asian merchandise imports to Singapore has been steadily increasing from around 55% in 1990 to 65% by 2005. The import shares for Singapore's key trading countries in Asia are given in Table 7. Singapore's neighbor, Malaysia,

---

[7]However Indonesia data must be taken with a pinch of salt as Singapore does not officially public bilateral trade with Indonesia. See Note in Table 6.

Table 4. Product Composition of Singapore's Merchandise Imports (%), 1994–2005

	Imports			
	1994	1999	2003	2005
Electrical & Electronic Components and Machinery	33.6	41.9	41.7	34.9
Manufactured Goods	10.6	8.0	6.8	7.5
Chemicals & Pharmaceutical	6.5	6.0	6.7	6.2
Fuels and Petroleum Products	8.8	9.1	13.6	17.8
Textiles & Clothing	2.0	1.1	1.0	0.3
Transport Equipment	22.8	18.3	17.4	20.9
Food, Beverages, Crude Materials	5.1	4.0	1.2	2.8
Miscellaneous Manufactures	10.6	11.6	11.6	9.6
Import of Goods (values S$)	$146,679m	$176,845m	$230,203m	$323,743m
Import of Services (values S$)	$34,210m	$31,998m	$69,187m	$90,349m
Transportation	25.8	33.3	33.5	36.6
Travel	17.4	24.6	20.1	18.1
Financial & Insurance	3.9	4.9	5.8	5.6
Other Services	52.9	37.2	40.6	39.7

Sources: Ministry of Trade and Industry, Economic Survey of Singapore, various issues; *Yearbook of Statistics*, Singapore, various issues.

has been a major source of imports, constituting about 14–15% of Singapore's total exports. Notably, Singapore's reliance on China for its imports has increased from 3.2% of total imports in 1995 to nearly 10% in 2005. The import share with India has also risen, albeit more slowly, from 0.7% in 1995 to over 2% in 2005. Figure 6 reveals that Singapore's imports have grown fastest in recent years from South Asia, suggesting further integration between the city state and South Asia, India in particular. These data only refer to merchandise trade. It is likely that Singapore's services trade with India has been rising fairly markedly.

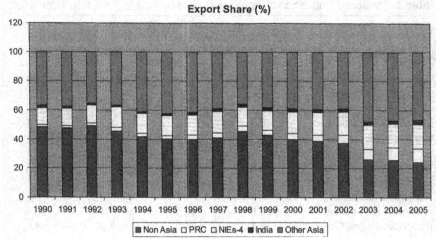

Source: ADB.

Fig. 3. Country Share of Singapore's Exports (%), 1990–2005.

Table 5. Direction of Singapore's Export (1991–2005)

	US$ million			Share in export (%)			Growth rate (%)		
	1991	1998	2005	1991	1998	2005	1991–1998	1998–2005	1991–2005
Asia	32,565	60,675	157,162	55.2	55.2	68.4	9.3	14.6	11.9
Bahrain	33	32	171	0.1	0.0	0.1	−0.5	27.1	12.5
Bangladesh	363	675	695	0.6	0.6	0.3	9.3	0.4	4.8
Brunei Darussalam	553	615	496	0.9	0.6	0.2	1.5	−3.0	−0.8
Cambodia	n.a.	296	303	n.a.	0.3	0.1	n.a.	0.3	n.a.
China, People's Rep. of	859	4,064	19,757	1.5	3.7	8.6	24.9	25.3	25.1
Hong Kong, China	4,252	9,221	21,522	7.2	8.4	9.4	11.7	12.9	12.3
India	1,000	2,436	5,893	1.7	2.2	2.6	13.6	13.5	13.5
Indonesia	n.a.	n.a.	22,103	n.a.	n.a.	9.6	n.a.	n.a.	n.a.
Iran	147	91	494	0.3	0.1	0.2	−6.6	27.3	9.0
Japan	5,114	7,231	12,532	8.7	6.6	5.5	5.1	8.2	6.6
Korea, Rep. of	1,394	2,566	8,052	2.4	2.3	3.5	9.1	17.7	13.3

(Continued)

Table 5. (*Continued*)

	US$ million			Share in export (%)			Growth rate (%)		
	1991	1998	2005	1991	1998	2005	1991–1998	1998–2005	1991–2005
Kuwait	50	65	102	0.1	0.1	0.0	3.6	6.7	5.1
Lao People's Dem. Rep.	n.a.	20	40	n.a.	0.0	0.0	n.a.	10.4	n.a.
Malaysia	8,818	16,746	30,385	15.0	15.2	13.2	9.6	8.9	9.2
Pakistan	262	313	646	0.4	0.3	0.3	2.6	10.9	6.7
Philippines	680	2,464	4,184	1.2	2.2	1.8	20.2	7.9	13.9
Saudi Arabia	453	382	425	0.8	0.3	0.2	−2.4	1.5	−0.5
Sri Lanka	231	524	681	0.4	0.5	0.3	12.4	3.8	8.0
Thailand	3,704	4,209	9,402	6.3	3.8	4.1	1.8	12.2	6.9
United Arab Emirates	599	1,025	3,695	1.0	0.9	1.6	8.0	20.1	13.9
Vietnam	n.a.	1,514	4,421	n.a.	1.4	1.9	n.a.	16.5	n.a.
America	13,307	24,383	29,044	22.6	22.2	12.6	9.0	2.5	5.7
Brazil	110	293	849	0.2	0.3	0.4	15.0	16.4	15.7
Canada	451	563	517	0.8	0.5	0.2	3.2	−1.2	1.0
United States	11,654	21,868	23,871	19.8	19.9	10.4	9.4	1.3	5.3
Europe	9,835	19,597	29,104	16.7	17.8	12.7	10.4	5.8	8.1
EU, of which	8,555	17,417	26,418	14.5	15.8	11.5	10.7	6.1	8.4
France	689	2,257	3,625	1.2	2.1	1.6	18.5	7.0	12.6
Germany	2,467	3,328	6,306	4.2	3.0	2.7	4.4	9.6	6.9
Italy	557	515	593	0.9	0.5	0.3	−1.1	2.0	0.4
Netherlands	1,516	3,787	5,480	2.6	3.4	2.4	14.0	5.4	9.6
Sweden	178	113	127	0.3	0.1	0.1	−6.3	1.6	−2.4
United Kingdom	1,784	3,730	6,318	3.0	3.4	2.8	11.1	7.8	9.5
Switzerland	447	1,128	668	0.8	1.0	0.3	14.1	−7.2	2.9
Oceania	1,968	3,809	11,819	3.3	3.5	5.1	9.9	17.6	13.7
Australia	1,456	3,155	8,432	2.5	2.9	3.7	11.7	15.1	13.4
New Zealand	189	368	1,163	0.3	0.3	0.5	10.0	17.9	13.9
Africa	1,276	1,439	2,522	2.2	1.3	1.1	1.7	8.3	5.0
Total	58,953	109,905	229,652	100.0	100.0	100.0	9.3	11.1	10.2

Source: United Nations Commodity Trade Statistics Database; authors' calculation.

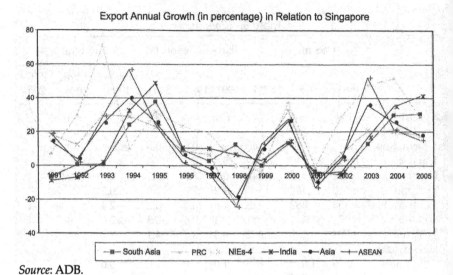

Source: ADB.

Fig. 4. Annual Growth of Singapore's Merchandise Exports to Asia, 1991–2005.

Table 6. Singapore's Export Markets in Asia: Share of Total Export, 1995–2005

Country	Exports % of total exports		
	1995	2000	2005
China	2.33	3.90	8.60
Hong Kong	8.57	7.86	9.37
Indonesia*	2.00	2.75	4.12
Japan	7.8	7.5	5.8
Malaysia	19.18	18.16	13.23
Philippines	1.63	2.45	1.82
South Korea	2.74	3.57	3.51
Thailand	5.77	4.26	4.09
Vietnam	1.51	1.52	1.93
Bangladesh	0.50	0.57	0.30
India	1.59	2.02	2.57
Pakistan	0.26	0.27	0.28
Sri Lanka	0.32	0.33	0.30

Note: *Indonesia's exports to Singapore are treated as Singapore imports from Indonesia. *Source:* United Nations Commodity Trade Statistics Online.

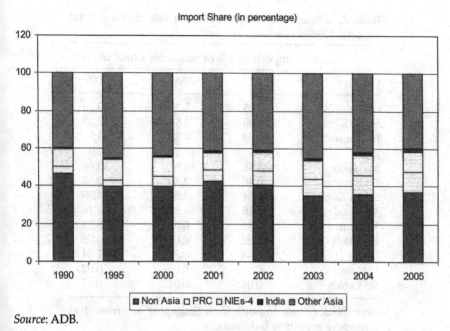

Source: ADB.

Fig. 5. Country Share of Singapore's Imports (%), 1990–2005.

Table 8 summarizes the top five exports of Singapore to the various Asian economies while Table 9 shows the share of exports by commodities (SITC classification) and by countries in Asia. Singapore's dynamic trade links with the Asian countries is apparent by three key export products: machines and transport equipments (SITC 7), mineral fuel (SITC 3) and chemical (SITC 5). The high share of trade in machines and transport equipments and chemicals reflects the linkages between the production structures of Singapore with the regional production network. The export share to China in machines and transport equipments (SITC 7) rose from 40% in 1995 to nearly 65% in 2005, while the export share in chemical (SITC 5) to China hovered around 15% in 1995–2005. In contrast, the export share of mineral fuel (SITC 3) and basic manufactures (SITC 6) has declined drastically over the years. As with China, Singapore's export to South Asia is mostly in machines and transport equipments and chemicals. The export share in machines and transport equipments to India

Table 7. Singapore's Import Sources in Asia: Share of Total Imports, 1995–2005

Country	Imports as a % of Singapore's total imports		
	1995	2000	2005
China	3.25	5.29	10.26
Hong Kong	3.30	2.61	2.10
Indonesia*	3.03	4.88	3.92
Japan	21.1	17.2	11.0
Malaysia	15.48	16.97	13.66
Philippines	0.88	2.50	2.32
South Korea	4.34	3.58	4.30
Thailand	5.16	4.31	3.76
Vietnam	0.36	0.61	0.91
Bangladesh	0.02	0.06	0.05
India	0.74	0.80	2.04
Pakistan	0.05	0.05	0.02
Sri Lanka	0.04	0.04	0.03

Note: *Indonesia's imports from Singapore are treated as Singapore exports to Indonesia.
Source: United Nations Commodity Trade Statistics Online.

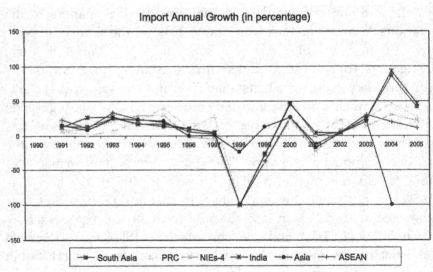

Import Annual Growth (in percentage)

— South Asia ⋯ PRC — NIEs-4 —✱— India —●— Asia —|— ASEAN

Source: ADB.

Fig. 6. Annual Growth of Singapore's Merchandise Imports from Asia, 1991–2005.

Table 8. Singapore's Top Five Exports to Various Asian Economies

Commodities	Value (S$ million)	Share (%)
Major Five Export Commodities to Brunei		
Civil Engg Eqpmt Parts	79	10
Telecommunications Equipment	36	4
Parts for Office & Dp Machines	25	3
Petroleum Products Refined	24	3
Motor Cars	23	3
Total	826	100
Major Five Export Commodities to Cambodia		
Petroleum Products Refined	179	35
Parts for Office & Dp Machines	31	6
Alcoholic Beverages	27	5
Tobacco Manufactures	22	4
Cloth Leather Machinery Parts	19	4
Total	505	100
Major Five Export Commodities to China		
Electronic Valves	11,002	33
Data Processing Machines	2,957	9
Petroleum Products Refined	2,478	8
Parts for Office & Dp Machines	2,359	7
Electrical Circuit Apparatus	804	2
Total	32,909	100
Major Five Export Commodities to Hong Kong		
Electronic Valves	13,476	38
Petroleum Products Refined	9,373	26
Data Processing Machines	1,782	5
Telecommunications Equipment	1,592	4
Parts for Office & Dp Machines	1,475	4
Total	35,849	100
Major Five Export Commodities to India		
Petroleum Products Refined	1,365	14
Parts for Office & Dp Machines	1,265	13
Data Processing Machines	854	9
Electronic Valves	573	6
Telecommunications Equipment	517	5
Total	9,817	100

(Continued)

Table 8. (*Continued*)

Commodities	Value (S$ million)	Share (%)
Major Five Export Commodities to Indonesia		
Petroleum Products Refined	5,844	16
Telecommunications Equipment	3,746	10
Parts for Office & Dp Machines	2,797	8
Civil Engg Eqpmt Parts	1,851	5
Electronic Valves	1,687	5
Total	36,817	100
Major Five Export Commodities to Japan		
Electronic Valves	6,342	30
Musical Instrument & Parts	1,824	9
Parts for Office & Dp Machines	1,702	8
Data Processing Machines	1,677	8
Petroleum Products Refined	1,349	6
Total	20,874	100
Major Five Export Commodities to Republic of Korea		
Electronic Valves	6,812	51
Parts for Office & Dp Machines	1,250	9
Data Processing Machines	497	4
Electrical Machinery Nes	305	2
Petroleum Products Refined	297	2
Total	13,412	100
Major Five Export Commodities to Laos		
Alcoholic Beverages	59	88
Tobacco Manufactures	2	4
Measuring Instruments	1	1
Data Processing Machines	1	1
Toys Garnes Etc	1	1
Total	67	100
Major Five Export Commodities to Malaysia		
Electronic Valves	15,566	31
Petroleum Products Refined	7,072	14
Parts for Office & Dp Machines	2,940	6
Telecommunications Equipment	2,851	6
Electrical Circuit Apparatus	2,204	4
Total	50,612	100

(*Continued*)

Table 8. (*Continued*)

Commodities	Value (S$ million)	Share (%)
Major Five Export Commodities to Myanmar		
Petroleum Products Refined	299	30
Civil Engg Eqpmt Parts	108	11
Milk & Cream	35	4
Articles of Paper	27	3
Parts for Office & Dp Machines	24	2
Total	991	100
Major Five Export Commodities to Philippines		
Petroleum Products Refined	1,432	21
Electronic Valves	1,321	19
Parts for Office & Dp Machines	557	8
Data Processing Machines	261	4
Electrical Circuit Apparatus	254	4
Total	6,969	100
Major Five Export Commodities to Taiwan		
Electronic Valves	7,664	51
Parts for Office & Dp Machines	697	5
Data Processing Machines	645	4
Telecommunications Equipment	593	4
Hydrocarbons Nes	509	3
Total	14,938	100
Major Five Export Commodities to Thailand		
Electronic Valves	2,779	18
Parts for Office & Dp Machines	1,458	9
Petroleum Products Refined	900	6
Musical Instrument & Parts	730	5
Telecommunications Equipment	708	5
Total	15,662	100
Major Five Export Commodities to Vietnam		
Petroleum Products Refined	3,637	49
Parts for Office & Dp Machines	264	4
Tobacco Manufactures	228	3
Data Processing Machines	210	3
Civil Engg Eqpmt Parts	169	2
Total	7,364	100

Source:

Table 9. Singapore Exports by SITC One-Digit Category as a % of Total Exports, 1995–2005

		SITC CATEGORY									
Country	Year	0	1	2	3	4	5	6	7	8	9
China	1995	1.53	1.63	2.79	18.27	1.52	13.07	13.19	40.07	3.63	4.31
	2000	0.71	0.18	1.99	13.31	0.08	14.66	4.56	57.57	6.13	0.81
	2005	0.50	0.45	1.21	7.76	0.02	14.97	2.56	65.45	5.91	1.16
Hong Kong	1995	1.75	2.26	0.79	18.46	0.43	6.08	4.31	57.04	7.89	0.99
	2000	1.07	0.82	0.42	21.86	0.04	6.21	3.41	58.71	5.99	1.46
	2005	0.60	0.17	0.29	24.76	0.01	5.26	2.12	60.50	4.28	2.01
Indonesia*	1995	0.97	0.13	5.60	34.33	0.95	21.18	5.95	25.39	5.49	0.01
	2000	1.06	0.02	2.05	45.53	0.22	19.72	9.12	19.99	2.29	0.00
	2005	1.59	0.08	1.11	69.07	0.11	12.16	4.31	10.35	1.22	0.00
Malaysia	1995	2.35	0.39	1.17	5.70	0.09	6.58	12.30	64.35	6.18	0.89
	2000	1.13	0.34	0.74	9.41	0.04	5.59	6.50	69.79	5.52	0.93
	2005	0.96	0.56	0.63	14.29	0.06	7.26	6.28	63.36	5.36	1.23
Philippines	1995	2.96	4.17	1.07	6.42	0.56	15.77	8.17	50.50	6.50	3.86
	2000	1.86	5.82	0.37	9.09	0.21	10.67	3.44	60.19	6.73	1.61
	2005	2.39	2.28	0.19	19.53	0.15	10.66	3.58	51.88	6.43	2.92
South Korea	1995	1.14	6.88	1.58	7.99	0.19	11.98	6.12	55.59	7.36	1.17
	2000	0.57	0.64	0.39	4.19	0.13	9.43	4.04	73.70	6.34	0.56
	2005	0.48	0.18	0.26	1.13	0.01	10.21	3.16	76.38	6.51	1.68
Thailand	1995	1.54	0.18	0.86	12.57	0.36	11.34	8.06	58.40	4.65	2.05
	2000	1.06	0.46	0.81	3.05	0.11	13.52	5.51	66.25	7.92	1.31
	2005	1.20	0.69	0.47	5.22	0.06	18.13	5.76	56.62	9.86	1.99
Vietnam	1995	1.93	12.51	0.65	34.68	0.78	9.84	9.51	25.12	4.09	0.89
	2000	0.73	7.90	0.52	43.73	0.05	9.82	5.59	25.15	5.83	0.68
	2005	0.83	4.17	0.48	50.45	0.10	10.88	5.35	22.98	3.49	1.26
Bangladesh	1995	2.48	0.75	2.28	41.32	1.04	8.57	17.66	19.27	5.68	0.97
	2000	1.36	0.64	0.71	35.39	0.81	12.15	10.71	29.95	8.15	0.12
	2005	3.19	0.49	4.27	6.13	0.17	18.39	8.25	49.13	8.42	1.55
India	1995	1.02	1.18	5.34	12.38	0.37	9.77	13.71	43.65	8.33	4.27
	2000	0.95	0.66	2.49	11.13	0.20	13.57	8.41	50.16	10.99	1.44
	2005	0.33	0.29	1.58	12.64	0.07	14.63	6.25	51.68	9.81	2.73
Pakistan	1995	3.82	0.47	6.91	0.41	0.97	26.87	13.73	36.09	8.28	2.46
	2000	3.78	0.16	2.03	2.01	0.50	21.86	9.81	48.88	10.73	0.23
	2005	1.25	0.25	0.86	3.07	0.28	25.73	8.14	50.28	9.45	0.70

(Continued)

Table 9. (*Continued*)

Country	Year	\	\	\	\	\	SITC CATEGORY	\	\	\	\
		0	1	2	3	4	5	6	7	8	9
Sri Lanka	1995	2.38	0.92	4.35	**4.09**	1.74	**16.62**	27.48	**29.48**	9.66	3.29
	2000	1.49	1.98	1.64	**11.55**	1.82	**14.33**	12.72	**39.47**	7.80	7.20
	2005	2.20	1.47	1.97	**17.81**	0.88	**13.83**	9.09	**39.58**	6.22	6.95

Note: *Indonesia's imports from Singapore are treated as Singapore exports to Indonesia.
SITC: 0 — Food & live animals; 1 — Beverages & Tobacco; 2 — Crude materials; 3 — Mineral fuel; 4 — Animal, vegetable oil, fat; 5 — Chemical; 6 — Basic manufactures; 7 — Machines, transport equipment; 8 — Miscellaneous manufactured goods; 9 — Goods not classified.
Source: United Nations Commodity Trade Statistics Online.

accounts for nearly 50% of Singapore's export's to that country. The export share of SITC 7 to Bangladesh increased from 19% in 1995 to over 49% in 2005. A similar trend is apparent for Pakistan, where the share increased from 36% in 1995 to nearly 50% in 2005.

The export shares of SITC 7 and SITC 5 to Korea and Hong Kong are also quite strong and indicate growing production linkages between these countries and Singapore. The export share of SITC 7 to Malaysia, Thailand and Philippines is more than 50% of the total exports to these countries. Indonesia is only exception in ASEAN, where the share of exports in SITC 7 declined from 25% in 1995 to only 10% in 2005. In contrast, the share of exports of SITC 3 (mineral fuels) increased from 34% in 1995 to 69% in 2005. Among the emerging ASEAN countries, Vietnam is becoming an important export destination for Singapore. The shares of export of SITC 7, SITC 3 and SITC 5 to Vietnam have increased significantly over the years.

Table 10 summarizes the top five imports of Singapore from the various Asian economies while Table 11 highlights the import shares by commodities and countries. The data indicate a different trade pattern compared to exports. Although the import share of SITC 7 (machines and transport equipments) is relatively high from Asian countries, the imports can be explained by its production linkages with the respective countries. Vietnam, Bangladesh, Pakistan

Table 10. Singapore's Top Five Imports from Asian Economies

Commodities	Value (S$ million)	Share (%)
Major Five Import Commodities from Brunei		
Apparel Articles of Textile	113	46
Women's Clothings Knitted	58	24
Petroleum Crude	34	14
Jewellery Etc	13	5
Special Transactions	10	4
Grand Total	248	100
Major Five Import Commodities from Cambodia		
Gold Non-monetary	61	37
Apparel Articles of Textile	31	18
Tobacco Manufactures	23	14
Women's Clothings Knitted	20	12
Women's Clothings Woven	17	10
Grand Total	167	100
Major Five Import Commodities from China		
Telecommunications Equipment	5,693	17
Electronic Valves	4,283	13
Parts for Office & Dp Machines	4,073	12
Data Processing Machines	2,980	9
Petroleum Products Refined	2,064	6
Grand Total	34,170	100
Major Five Import Commodities from Hong Kong		
Electronic Valves	1,614	23
Telecommunications Equipment	887	13
Parts for Office & Dp Machines	673	10
Electrical Machinery Nes	501	7
Jewellery Etc	367	5
Grand Total	7,009	100
Major Five Import Commodities from India		
Precious Stones & Pearls	2,738	40
Petroleum Products Refined	1,802	27
Aluminium	247	4
Jewellery Etc	180	3
Hydrocarbons Nes	130	2
Grand Total	6,788	100

(Continued)

Table 10. (*Continued*)

Commodities	Value (S$ million)	Share (%)
Major Five Import Commodities from Indonesia		
Parts for Office & Dp Machines	2,267	13
Petroleum Products Refined	1,954	11
Electronic Valves	1,245	7
Data Processing Machines	982	6
Telecommunications Equipment	941	5
Grand Total	17,400	100
Major Five Import Commodities from Japan		
Electronic Valves	6,894	22
Telecommunications Equipment	2,114	7
Parts for Office & Dp Machines	1,874	6
Electrical Machinery Nes	1,427	4
Specialized Machinery Nes	1,238	4
Grand Total	32,034	100
Major Five Import Commodities from Republic of Korea		
Electronic Valves	7,248	51
Telecommunications Equipment	2,081	15
Petroleum Products Refined	935	7
Motor Cars	302	2
Parts for Office & Dp Machines	221	2
Grand Total	14,323	100
Major Five Import Commodities from Laos		
Copper	1	54
Coffee	0.4	17
Wood Shaped or Worked	0.3	11
Men's Clothings Woven	0.2	10
Prefabricated Buildings	0.1	3
Grand Total	2	100
Major Five Import Commodities from Malaysia		
Electronic Valves	14,757	32
Parts for Office & Dp Machines	5,462	12
Telecommunications Equipment	3,686	8
Petroleum Products Refined	2,751	6
Data Processing Machines	1,503	3
Grand Total	45,527	100

(*Continued*)

Table 10. (*Continued*)

Commodities	Value (S$ million)	Share (%)
Major Five Import Commodities from Myanmar		
Petroleum Crude	79	44
Crustaceans Etc Fresh Dried	26	14
Wood Shaped or Worked	17	9
Tobacco Manufactures	8	4
Vegetables Fresh Chilled Etc	8	4
Total	180	100
Major Five Import Commodities from Philippines		
Electronic Valves	5,137	66
Parts for Office & Dp Machines	520	7
Data Processing Machines	352	5
Petroleum Crude	289	4
Petroleum Products Refined	281	4
Total	7,742	100
Major Five Import Commodities from Taiwan		
Electronic Valves	12,883	65
Petroleum Products Refined	1,760	9
Parts for Office & Dp Machines	821	4
Telecommunications Equipment	539	3
Electrical Circuit Apparatus	432	2
Total	19,720	100
Major Five Import Commodities from Thailand		
Petroleum Products Refined	2,483	20
Parts for Office & Dp Machines	2,287	18
Electronic Valves	1,561	12
Data Processing Machines	877	7
Motor Cars	408	3
Total	12,516	100
Major Five Import Commodities from Vietnam		
Petroleum Crude	2,417	80
Footwear	97	3
Data Processing Machines	50	2
Fish Fresh Chilled Frozen	31	1
Electrical Circuit Apparatus	22	1
Total	3,026	100

Table 11. Singapore Imports by SITC One-Digit Category as a % of Total Imports, 1995–2005

		SITC CATEGORY									
Country	Year	0	1	2	3	4	5	6	7	8	9
China	1995	8.05	3.23	1.96	5.36	0.06	4.01	**25.53**	**39.99**	**11.54**	0.29
	2000	3.25	0.63	0.64	8.09	0.04	2.91	**11.42**	**60.96**	**11.86**	0.20
	2005	1.55	0.42	0.31	6.51	0.07	2.53	**8.87**	**69.27**	**10.13**	0.34
Hong Kong	1995	1.23	1.57	0.28	0.21	0.01	1.88	7.94	**62.31**	**23.18**	1.38
	2000	1.19	0.09	0.23	0.37	0.01	2.53	6.65	**63.20**	**24.85**	0.88
	2005	0.59	0.75	0.51	0.01	0.00	2.06	6.10	**68.71**	**20.83**	0.45
Indonesia*	1995	8.47	0.28	8.82	**16.61**	0.37	1.89	**18.88**	**29.83**	13.92	0.91
	2000	5.50	0.18	2.47	**11.96**	1.21	3.35	**14.30**	**49.21**	8.12	3.71
	2005	4.18	0.75	3.03	**10.49**	2.27	3.40	**17.44**	**53.01**	4.41	1.02
Malaysia	1995	4.40	0.18	3.04	**4.78**	2.44	1.84	7.58	**64.01**	**11.56**	0.18
	2000	2.78	0.52	2.04	**3.39**	0.79	2.53	6.06	**71.93**	**9.80**	0.15
	2005	2.65	0.41	0.94	**9.01**	0.83	3.32	5.67	**67.81**	**9.11**	0.25
Philippines	1995	2.96	0.03	1.40	1.47	0.69	0.73	5.64	**79.36**	3.26	4.44
	2000	0.52	0.13	0.35	1.64	0.00	0.34	1.10	**93.74**	1.74	0.44
	2005	0.53	0.22	0.85	7.40	0.00	0.36	0.92	**87.41**	2.18	0.12
South Korea	1995	0.68	0.02	0.26	0.89	0.00	2.48	10.95	**80.97**	3.54	0.19
	2000	0.60	0.02	0.87	6.59	0.01	2.74	9.80	**75.45**	3.32	0.60
	2005	0.24	0.07	0.20	6.73	0.01	3.88	7.27	**78.97**	2.04	0.60
Thailand	1995	4.66	0.22	1.74	**1.15**	0.05	1.18	6.31	**80.94**	3.61	0.13
	2000	5.04	0.20	1.27	**10.83**	0.01	2.74	6.05	**70.60**	3.17	0.09
	2005	3.64	0.20	1.58	**19.96**	0.06	5.51	6.52	**58.08**	4.00	0.46
Vietnam	1995	**33.19**	0.05	9.88	**40.45**	0.08	2.03	2.75	5.20	6.11	0.26
	2000	**13.27**	0.53	1.95	**67.91**	0.00	0.78	2.33	5.86	7.11	0.24
	2005	**3.91**	0.67	0.45	**80.07**	0.00	0.73	2.43	5.52	5.92	0.29
Bangladesh	1995	**21.48**	0.00	0.04	**25.31**	0.00	0.87	14.03	8.13	**28.87**	1.29
	2000	**2.61**	0.10	0.03	**5.99**	0.01	0.58	2.94	8.05	**78.52**	1.17
	2005	**1.99**	0.46	0.07	**37.29**	0.01	0.44	2.23	5.57	**50.63**	1.31
India	1995	**10.21**	0.16	4.38	**1.84**	0.30	9.14	**37.80**	**24.09**	**11.81**	0.27
	2000	**5.86**	0.50	2.63	**9.81**	0.05	11.91	**29.98**	**26.90**	**11.85**	0.51
	2005	**1.79**	0.24	1.42	**26.55**	0.03	6.93	**49.89**	**6.90**	**5.93**	0.32
Pakistan	1995	**11.48**	0.00	2.18	**0.00**	0.00	**2.50**	66.58	2.89	**12.64**	1.74
	2000	**10.33**	0.03	0.65	35.29	0.00	**4.95**	35.01	2.15	**11.48**	0.12
	2005	**15.48**	1.41	1.45	17.66	0.00	**15.45**	25.66	5.12	**16.87**	0.91

(Continued)

Table 11. *(Continued)*

Country	Year	0	1	2	3	4	5	6	7	8	9
					SITC CATEGORY						
Sri Lanka	1995	24.47	0.14	6.74	8.67	0.10	2.08	10.04	31.01	15.55	1.20
	2000	24.04	0.30	1.09	25.84	0.15	2.61	10.59	25.39	8.82	1.18
	2005	18.43	3.39	1.52	0.00	0.00	6.16	11.83	45.53	12.53	0.60

Note: *Indonesia's exports to Singapore are treated as Singapore imports from Indonesia.
SITC: 0 — Food & live animals; 1 — Beverages & Tobacco; 2 — Crude materials; 3 — Mineral fuel; 4 — Animal, vegetable oil, fat; 5 — Chemical; 6 — Basic manufactures; 7 — Machines, transport equipment; 8 — Miscellaneous manufactured goods; 9 — Goods not classified.
Source: United Nations Commodity Trade Statistics Online.

and Sri Lanka are important sources of imports by Singapore of agricultural food products and live animals. Although, Indonesia, Thailand, Vietnam and South Asian countries provide mineral fuels for Singapore's manufacturing. Singapore's linkage to the production chain in Asia is reflected by the import share of SITC 7 to the ASEAN countries. The import share of machines and transport equipments is more than 60% of the total imports from Indonesia, Malaysia, Philippines, and Thailand in 2005. These countries are important conduits for the integration of the value-chain in South-East Asia. Singapore is also strongly linked to the East Asian countries of South Korea and Hong Kong with a share of import of SITC 7 of nearly 65% and 78% respectively. It is also interesting to observe that the share of imports of machines and transport equipments from China rose from 40% in 1995 to nearly 70% in 2005.

Chapter 4

Trade and Investment Related Infrastructure and Policies

4.1. Import Protection and Export Promotion

Singapore has embraced a policy of free trade and has imposed very few border measures. Most of the measures imposed at the border are for health, security and environmental reasons. Singapore imposes negligible tariffs, with only six tariff lines subject to specific rates of duty (WTO, 2004). The exception is the import of rice which is subjected to import licensing for security reasons. The other charges that are imposed on imports is the goods and services tax (GST) of 5% which applies to most imports and also excise tax on alcohol, petroleum, tobacco products, and motor vehicles.

While customs clearance for most goods is automatic with minimal administrative delays (see Section 4.2), certain imports such as fresh and processed food products are required to be registered with Customs as well as the Agri-Food and Veterinary Authority (AVA). The government also provides exemption from import duty and GST for goods that are temporarily imported for re-exports within three months of imports. The Customs also permits imports that are used as intermediate inputs in production to be eligible for exemption from custom duties and excise tax. In addition, the

45

Customs imposes non-tariff restrictions such as quantity/quota restrictions on certain products for health, security and environmental reasons. There are quantitative restrictions on chewing gum (except for oral and medicinal chewing gums), certain cosmetics, imports of used motor vehicles more than three years old, telecommunication equipment such as military communication equipment, etc. The details of the tariff and non-tariff barriers imposed by the Singapore government are given in the Annexes 2 and 3, respectively.

Singapore does not apply any export levies or taxes. However, all exporters registered under the Companies Act or Business Registration Act are required to be registered with the Customs electronically (see Section 4.2). All traders exporting strategic goods such as arms, chemicals and biological materials and nuclear-related products are required to seek approval from the Customs by applying for valid permits prior to export. Permits are also required for exports of certain products subject to quotas, such as textiles and clothing to certain markets, and safety and health documents are also required for agricultural products. Export restrictions are maintained mainly for health and security reasons that involve animals, animal products, fish and fish products, arms and explosives, chemical and radioactive products.

The Singapore government provides extensive tax concessions and exemptions to companies engaged in international trade through the government statutory broad, International Enterprise Singapore (IE) to encourage and promote trade. Under the Global Trader Programme (GTP), approved companies are granted a concessionary tax rate of 10% on international trading activities. In the International Shipping Enterprise Incentive scheme (AIS), approved international shipping companies are given tax exemptions for ten years on income from qualifying shipping operations (Table 1). IE Singapore also provides incentives for local companies to venture overseas and to establish strong regional and global trade links through the Overseas Investment Incentive Scheme and Regionalization Finance Scheme.

Table 1. Incentives to Promote Trade in Singapore

Scheme	Eligibility	Incentive
Global Trader Programme	International companies that are involved in international trade, procurement, marketing and distribution of qualifying commodities and products	Concessionary tax rates on international trading activities in approved commodities and products.
Approved International Shipping Enterprise Incentive (AIS)	International shipping companies with worldwide networks.	Tax exemptions for ten years on income from qualifying shipping operations.
Approved Cyber Trader Programme (ACT)	Companies conducting international business through the use of internet.	Concessionary tax rate of 10% of qualifying offshore income on qualifying products.
Double Tax Deduction for Market Development (DTD)	All Singapore registered companies with the primary purpose of promoting the trade in goods and services.	Deduction against taxable income of twice the eligible expenses incurred in approved activities as covered under Section 14B of the Income Tax Act.
Double deduction for overseas investment development expenditure	Manufacturing and services companies	Double deduction for qualifying expenditure incurred in approved feasibility studies and maintenance of overseas project offices against income.
Overseas Investment Incentive	All Singapore registered companies	Companies may defer income tax payments from their profitable operations in Singapore for two years if their approved overseas investment incurs operating losses during the first three years of investment.

(Continued)

Table 1. (*Continued*)

Scheme	Eligibility	Incentive
Regionalization Finance Scheme	Singapore registered company with 51% local equity and fixed productive asset of not more than S$30 m. If the company is involved in the services sector, it must employ not more than 200 employees.	Fixed-cost financing programme designed to assist local enterprises to globalize their operations. Fixed-rate loans are available under the scheme for acquiring fixed assets for overseas projects.

Source: WTO (2004).

4.2. Other Trade Enhancing Infrastructures

4.2.1. *Customs Clearance*

The Singapore Customs maintains an electronic infrastructure that reduces transaction cost in permit applications and seamlessly allow greater flow of goods and services across the border. Importers and exporters are required to adhere to the custom procedures of registering under the Business Registration Act or either as company registered under the Companies Act. All importers and exporters are required to apply for a Central Registration number (CR) from the Singapore customs, which allows the customs to electronically interface with the relevant parties through electronic system known as TradeNet. The CR number allows importers and exporters to submit all required trade permits electronically through the TradeNet, which allows a single application to be cleared by both Customs and the relevant government agencies. Payment of duties, GST, and other fees are directly deducted from the Trader's bank account, which reduces the transaction cost of cheques and other enforcements (see Table 2). For sea shipments, shipping agents use Manifest Reconciliation Statement (MRS). Traders report their warehouse inventory through Warehouse Inventory Submission Electronically via Internet (WISE) for dutiable goods and Petrolink for petroleum products. Together

Table 2. Singapore's Approach to Customs Procedures in 2004

Section	Current activities/Measures
Greater Public Availability of Information,	Singapore's Customs Act and its subsidiary legislation, as well as the Regulation of Imports and Exports Act and its subsidiary legislation, are available on the Internet and for sale to the public. Information on administrative regulations and procedures are also made available via brochures, circulars, helplists, guide books, Call Center and and on the Customs, TradeNet^{TM} as well as Strategic Goods Control Internet websites. Information on customs procedures can be found at http://www.customs.gov.sg. Information on the TradeNet^{TM} system can be found at http://www.tradenet.gov.sg. Information on strategic goods control system can be found at http://www.stgc.gov.sg. Singapore has in place an advance ruling system. Singapore Customs has a unit which attends to requests for advance rulings regarding classification of goods, rules of origin, etc. Advance rulings are made available as FAQs, circulars and help lists on the Singapore Customs website. Singapore has in place an open system for appeals. Businesses can approach Singapore Customs directly in writing, in person or over the telephone for appeal on decisions and seek clarification or redress. They can also appeal against decisions on procedures at regular dialogue sessions or write to the Ministry of Finance for assistance and advice. Inquiry contact points to the various branches of Singapore Customs are provided on its website. The updating of information (disseminated through various channels) on customs procedures is an on-going process.
Paperless trading	Singapore utilizes IT extensively in its customs and trade operations. Currently, nearly 100% of all customs and trade declarations are submitted electronically through the TradeNet^{TM} system, which complies with the UN/EDIFACT standards. When the declaration is approved by Customs, duties and GST assessed on the declaration will be electronically deducted via Inter-Bank GIRO (IBG).

(Continued)

Table 2. (*Continued*)

Section	Current activities/Measures
	A paperless system has also been implemented for the clearance of containerised cargo at all checkpoints.
Provision of Temporary Importation Facilities	Singapore provides various facilities for temporary importation. Singapore has been a contracting party to the Convention on the A.T.A. Carnet for the Temporary Admission of Goods (A.T.A. Convention) since 1983. Goods, except tobacco products and liquors, can be imported under the Temporary Import Scheme for repairs, trade exhibitions, displays and other approved purposes without payment of duty and/or Goods and Services Tax (GST). Bona fide trade samples can also be imported without payment of duty and/or GST. Since 2002, Singapore Customs has also accepted insurance bonds, in addition to bank guarantee, as a form of security for temporarily imported goods.
Implementation of Clear Appeals Provisions	Singapore has in place an open system for appeals. Businesses can approach Singapore Customs directly in writing, in person or over the telephone for appeal on decisions and seek clarification or redress. They can also appeal against decisions on procedures at regular dialogue sessions or write to the Ministry of Finance for assistance and advice.
Alignment with WTO Valuation Agreement	Singapore implemented the WTO Customs Valuation Agreement on 17 October 1997, three years ahead of schedule.
Adoption of Kyoto Convention	Singapore is in the process of studying the Revised Kyoto Convention with a view of aligning its customs procedures and practices with the provisions of the revised Kyoto Convention.
Implementation of Harmonised System Convention	Singapore has been adopting the Harmonised System for the classification of goods since 1 January 1989. Singapore implemented the 1996 version of the HS on 1 January 1996 and the HS 2002 amendments on 1 Jan 2002. Singapore implemented the ASEAN Harmonised Tariff Nomenclature (AHTN) on 1 Jan 2003. The Harmonised Codes are standardised at 8-digit level for use by all ASEAN countries. The purpose of the AHTN is to promote consistency, predictability and uniform interpretation in the classification of goods, and to facilitate trade among the ten ASEAN countries.

(*Continued*)

Table 2. (*Continued*)

Section	Current activities/Measures
Implementation of an Advance Classification Ruling System	Singapore has in place an advance classification ruling system. Singapore Customs has a Classification Section which attends to enquiries on the classification of goods. Classification certificates are issued upon request.
Implementation of the TRIPs Agreement	Singapore's IPR regime pertaining to border enforcement is compliant with the TRIPS Agreement.
Development of a Compendium of Harmonised Trade Data Elements	Singapore is studying the WCO Data Model sets against its own data requirements for customs and trade documentation. Singapore is also in the process of reviewing the structure and integrating certain aspects of the TradeNet™ system to remove excessive fields to facilitate trade declarations.
Adoption of Systematic Risk Management Techniques	Singapore has implemented risk management in the cargo and passenger clearance operations. Radiographic inspection systems have also been deployed at the port areas since 2003 to allow containers to be inspected quickly and to improve the detection capability of border enforcement agencies.
Implementation of WCO Guidelines on Express Consignment Clearance	Singapore has an efficient electronic system known as the Advance Clearance for Courier and Express Shipments (ACCESS) for the clearance of express consignments.
Integrity	Singapore has put in place stringent standards to ensure high level of integrity among its officers. Singapore Customs officers and border enforcement officers are briefed on integrity matters upon joining the civil service. Officers are also required to submit mandatory declarations of investments, assets and indebtedness annually. Singapore Customs is also subjected to internal and external audit checks. An anti-corruption legislation, Prevention of Corruption Act, is also in place, and is enforced by the Corrupt Practices Investigation Bureau.

(*Continued*)

Table 2. (*Continued*)

Section	Current activities/Measures
Customs-Business Partnership	This CAP was established in Feb 2002. Singapore has in-place, official liaison channels with businesses and trade associations, in the form of outreach sessions, trade consultations, regular dialogue sessions and the Customs Advisory Committee, among others, to foster a better working relationship, which would result in (i) obtaining feedback to improve the government's requirements and procedures; and (ii) enhancing communication and co-operation between Customs and the business sector.
	Singapore has contributed four programmes, namely ACCESS, dialogue sessions with trade, Customs Advisory Committee and Customs Documentation Course, to the Compendium on "Best Practices on Customs-Business Partnership" compiled by Hong Kong Customs.

Source: http://www.apec-iap.org.

with the Economic Development Board (EDB) and Infocomm Development Authority (IDA), Singapore Customs also launched TradeXchange which offers an integrated electronic system of "workflow, submissions and enquiries to the Sea Ports, Airports, Maritime Authorities, Customs and Controlling Agencies".

Singapore also offers Free Trade Zones (FTZ), Licensed Warehouses, and Export Processing Zone (EPZ). FTZs facilitate entrepot trade in dutiable goods in which traders may repackage, sort, re-condition, and store their goods (except for liquors and cigarettes). In Licensed Warehouses, traders may store liquors, tobacco products, motor vehicles, and other goods that subject to GST. Under the Land Transport Authority's EPZ scheme, for example, traders may keep their de-registered vehicles pending export for upto 12 months.

4.2.2. *Infrastructure to Facilitate Labor Mobility*

Singapore boasts among the world's fastest clearance at checkpoints for labor flows. Thanks to the Immigration Automated Clearance

System (IACS), which uses biometrics and smart card technologies, frequent travellers may enjoy speedy immigration clearance through automated lanes at checkpoints. Because Singapore participates in the Asia-Pacific Economic Cooperation (APEC) Business Travel Card (ABTC) scheme which facilitates the travel of business persons between APEC countries, ABTC cardholders may also pass through designated ABTC lanes. Moreover, under the Dual-Channel System at all entry checkpoints — Red Channel for those who carry controlled or taxable items, and Green Channel for those who do not — travellers who have nothing to declare may proceed to the Green Channel for faster clearance.

4.2.3. *Infrastructure to Facilitate FDI*

Despite being one of the most competitive economies in the world, Singapore is constantly striving to cut red tape. Online Application System for Integrated Services (OASIS), a cross-agency project that spans more than 30 government agencies, through its Online Business Licensing Service (OBLS), offers on average an eight-day business license processing time. The Ministry of Trade and Industry's Pro-Enterprise Panel actively solicits feedback to remove rules and regulations that hamper businesses. Action Community for Entrepreneurship (ACE), collaboration between the private and government sectors, also facilitates debates on the business rule and regulation.

Singapore offers a good environment for high-technology- and information-technology MNCs. Singapore has strong Intellectual Property Rights (IPR) protection. To resolve disputes in a new frontier like e-commerce, Singapore Subordinate Courts offer Alternative Dispute Resolution. To promote healthy competition among firms in the market, the newly established Competition Commission of Singapore administers and enforces the Competition Act.

Singapore also supports R&D-related businesses. Singapore Science Park provides the infrastructure in its three science parks. Agency for Science, Technology and Research (A*Star) — through, among others, it's Fusionopolis (information and media industries) and Biopolis (biomedical sciences industry) — fosters scientific research in Singapore.

4.2.4. *Other Government E-Services*

Singapore Government offers various e-services to facilitate paperwork. Singapore Customs, for example, allows applications for registration, permits, or license to be submitted electronically. At Immigration & Checkpoints Authority, applicants can extend Social Visit Pass and apply for visa or student pass online. Through the Inland Revenue Authority of Singapore's myTax Portal, taxpayers may file and pay their taxes online.

Chapter 5

Services Trade Policies and Issues

Singapore is a major exporter of services accounting for nearly 2% of total global trade in services and ranked within the top 20 services exporting countries in the world (Table 1).

The export composition of services trade in Singapore was noted in Chapter 3. The transport services accounts for nearly 40% of the total export of services accounts for the Singapore economy. Given the world-class aviation hub in Singapore with Singapore Airlines and leading sector in Port services, the logistics and aviation sector remains an important services sector for the Singapore economy. However, the share of the transport services is declining over the years, falling to nearly 35% in 2005 from 53% in 1994. The financial services is emerging as a strong sector for services export, rising to nearly 9.4% in 2005 from 1% in 1994 of total trade in services.

Given the liberalization of the financial sector in 1999 that removed the barriers for foreign banks to set up full-licensed banks in Singapore, the financial sector is expected to grow further in the future. The key focus of the liberalization is to position Singapore as a leading international financial center by attracting more global banks and foreign investments in the services sector. The other important sector that has also been subjected to liberalization is the telecommunication sector. In 2000, the government lifted the foreign equity ownership limits in the telecommunication sector and allowed greater competition in the telecommunication services. Temasek, the major

Table 1. Singapore's Position in Global Trade in Commercial Services, 2005

Rank	Exporters	Value (US$ billion)	Share in World total (%)	Rank	Importers	Value (US$ billion)	Share in World total (%)
1	United States	354.0	14.7	1	United States	281.2	12.0
2	United Kingdom	188.7	7.8	2	Germany	201.4	8.6
3	Germany	148.5	6.2	3	United Kingdom	154.1	6.6
4	France	115.0	4.8	4	Japan	132.6	5.6
5	Japan	107.9	4.5	5	France	104.9	4.5
6	Italy	93.5	3.9	6	Italy	92.4	3.9
7	Spain	92.7	3.8	7	China	83.2	3.5
8	Netherlands	76.7	3.2	8	Netherlands	70.9	3.0
9	China	73.9	3.1	9	Ireland	66.1	2.8
10	Hong Kong, China	62.2	2.6	10	Spain	65.2	2.8
11	India	56.1	2.3	11	Canada	64.2	2.7
12	Ireland	53.3	2.2	12	Korea, Republic of	57.7	2.5
13	Belgium	53.3	2.2	13	India	52.2	2.2
14	Austria	52.6	2.2	14	Belgium	50.3	2.1
15	Canada	52.2	2.2	15	Austria	48.5	2.1
16	**Singapore**	**45.1**	**1.9**	16	**Singapore**	**44.0**	**1.9**
24	Australia	27.7	1.1	22	Australia	28.9	1.2
28	Thailand	20.5	0.8	23	Thailand	27.5	1.2
29	Malaysia	19.0	0.8	27	Indonesia*	23.2	1.0
				29	Malaysia	21.6	0.9
	World	2,415.0	100.0		World	2,345.0	100.0

Note: *Secretariat estimate.
Source: International Trade Statistics 2006, WTO.

shareholder of SingTel, announced a reduction of its shareholding from 67% to 5% in 2004.

Under the General Agreement on Trade in Services (GATS), Singapore has made commitments in business services, communication services, construction services, financial services, tourism and travel related services, and transport services. Under its Schedule of Commitments, market access for natural persons are unbound, except for the temporary movement of intra-corporate transfers of personnel up to three years, extending for another two years.

Foreigners registering their companies in Singapore are subjected to commercial presence restrictions. However, Most Favoured Nation (MFN) exemptions applies for the following: preference for workers from traditional source of supply, investment guarantees against unforeseen contingencies (such as war, etc) only for signatories of Investment Guarantee Agreement with Singapore, and tax relief for income derived from a Commonwealth country (see WTO, 2004). Further exemptions are given for several services sectors that include legal services, broadcasting, maritime transport, insurance, banking and other financial services. Table 2 outlines Singapore's general approach to trade in services and its multilateral commitments in the services sector.

Table 2. Singapore's Approach to Trade in Services in 2004

Section	Current entry requirements
Foreign Investment or Right of Establishment (including Joint Venture Requirements)	Commercial Presence is generally unrestricted. Subject to notification and the following residency requirement, all forms of commercial presence are allowed in Singapore: • Business — One manager who is either a Singapore citizen, Singapore permanent resident, or Singapore Employment Pass holder ("a local resident"). *Note*: Employment Passes are essentially permits allowing foreigners to work in Singapore. • Branch — Two agents who are local residents • Local Company — one director who is a local resident
Temporary Entry and Stay of Service Providers and Intra-Corporate Transferees	Managers, executives, and specialists employed by foreign corporations (at least one year preceding the application for entry) may freely be transferred into local offices or affiliates in Singapore. They will be granted entry for a two-year period, which may be extended for up to three additional years. Entry is subject to the usual immigration requirements. In the areas listed below, there are no restrictions on trade other than horizontal measures (commercial presence and entry of natural persons) as outlined above: • Veterinary services • Dental services

(Continued)

Table 2. (*Continued*)

Section	Current entry requirements
	• Library services
	• Interior design services excluding architecture
	• Software implementation services
	• Data processing services
	• Database services
	• Information technology consultancy services
	• Advertising services
	• Market research and public opinion polling services
	• Management consulting services
	• Public relations consultancy services
	• Biotechnology services
	• Services incidental to agriculture, hunting and forestry
	• Services incidental to fishing
	• Services incidental to mining
	• Building-cleaning services
	• Translation/interpretation services
	• Motion picture and video tape production and distribution services
	• Motion picture projection services
	• Sound recording services
	• General construction work for buildings
	• General construction work for civil engineering
	• Installation and assembly work
	• Building completion and finishing work
	• Hotel [FN2] and restaurant services (FN2 Cross-border supply in terms of market access is unbound due to lack of technical feasibility)
	• Travel agent and tour operator services
	• Tourist guide services
	• Economic and behavioral research
	• Industrial research
	• Freight transportation less cabotage
	• Shipping brokerage
	• Shipping agency
Foreign Exchange Control/Movement of Capital	Singapore lifted all controls on foreign exchange since 1978

Source: http://www.apec-iap.org

Bilateral trade accords, particularly the recent ones Singapore is involved in, go well beyond just merchandise trade liberalization, also encompassing liberalization of services trade and other "behind the border" impediments to trade and investment flows. In other words, they include trade and investment facilitation measures such as investment protection, harmonization and mutual recognition of standards and certification, protection of intellectual property rights, opening of government procurement markets, streamlining and harmonization of customs procedures and the development of dispute settlement procedures. Such trade accords which focus on "deep" integration could help establish a precedent or benchmark for multilateral trade negotiations. Simultaneously, to the extent that contracting parties to a trade accord agree to move beyond their respective WTO commitments, there may be a demonstration effect that motivates future rounds of broader multilateral negotiations under the auspices of the WTO (Rajan and Sen, 2002).

Singapore's trade pacts go beyond the GATS commitments that include financial services, business and professional services, telecommunications, education, and environmental services. For instance, trade in services is the main component of US-Singapore FTA, where there is substantial market access to the services sectors subject to a "negative list" that deals with sensitive government institutions and policy.

No doubt, that compared to multilateral agreements, bilateral agreements are weaker avenues to reduce trade barriers across countries (Thangavelu and Toh, 2005; Toh, 2006). However, given the recent failures of trade talks at WTO, bilateral agreements could form an important conduit for trade negotiations which could not be agreed through a multilateral setting. Singapore takes pains to highlight that its FTAs are WTO-plus in the sense that they go beyond the agreements that are required by the WTO. To emphasize this point, the following quote by Roy *et al* (2006) is worth reproducing:

> (O)ne of the leaders in propagating services (F)TAs, Singapore has followed a positive-list approach with India, EFTA, New Zealand and Japan, and a negative-list approach in its (F)TAs with the US, Korea and Australia. The commitments it has taken in the latter three agreements tend to go

further than the others, especially the (F)TA with the US and, to a lesser extent, that with Australia. There is, overall, much diversity in the commitments undertaken by Singapore in its various (F)TAs. Examples of (F)TA commitments going beyond the GATS schedule/offer include: new commitments, although with various limitations, on legal services (only for the US and Australia), including with additional explicit phase-in liberalization in the (F)TA with the US; new and improved commitments for various sub-sectors under "Business Services"; new commitments on courier services (except in the (F)TAs with India and Korea) and on maritime freight transport, as well as some other services relating to maritime transport; improvements to commitments on basis telecom (no ownership restriction for facilities based services) in most (F)TAs; new commitments on retailing services in all (F)TAs, although limits attached vary; new commitments on a number of air transport services, depending on the (F)TA; and a number of improved commitments in financial services (e.g. removal of foreign equity limits on insurance), including explicit phase-in liberalization in (F)TA with the US (pp. 23–24).

Beyond goods and services trade, Singapore's FTAs has also committed to promote competition by addressing anti-competitive practices through legislature is a key provision in the US-Singapore and Singapore-Australia FTAs (Table 3). This law is expected to apply to all activities including the private sector and Government Linked Corporations (GLCs) in all sectors, unless there are exclusions and exemptions for reasons of public policy and interest. Singapore has also actively engaged in efforts to improve corporate governance through voluntary Code of Corporate Governance for all listed companies. Specifically, a Council on Corporate Disclosure and Governance was established in 2002 to prescribe and strengthen existing accounting standards, disclosure practices, and reporting standards in Singapore.

Due to the FTAs with Australia, European Union, New Zealand and United States, there have significant changes in the framework of intellectual property rights (IPRs) in Singapore. For example, Singapore extends copyright protection to the life of the author plus 70 years, measures against the circumvention of technologies that protect copyright works, imposes protection of well known marks, and an extension of the patent term for pharmaceuticals because of the delays in marketing approval (WTO-plus TPE Singapore 2004). Further, Singapore has acceded to some international agreements

Table 3. Elements of Selected FTAs Negotiated by Singapore

Agreement/ Sector	ANZSCEP	JSEPA	ESFTA	SAFTA	USSFTA
	Agreement between Singapore and New Zealand on a Closer Economic Partnership, in force since January 2001. To be reviewed biannually.	Agreement between Singapore and Japan for a New-Age Economic Partnership in force since November 2002. To be reviewed annually.	Agreement between Singapore and EFTA states in force since January 2003. To be reviewed biannually.	Agreement between Singapore and Australia in force since July 2003. To be reviewed annually.	Agreement between Singapore and the United States in force since January 2004. To be reviewed annually.
Goods	Elimination of customs duties on date of entry into force.	Singapore eliminated all remaining customs duties on imports from Japan on entry into force. Based on a positive list. For most exports to Japan, tariff elimination is immediate. For the rest, tariff elimination is phased over a $3\frac{1}{2}$ to eight-year period.	Elimination of duties on industrial goods on entry into force. Liberalization of duties on agricultural goods based on positive list and on agreements with each EFTA state; duties on processed agricultural and fish products to be liberalized based on positive lists with each EFTA state.	Elimination of customs duties on entry into force.	Based on a positive list. Singapore eliminated all remaining customs duties on imports from the United States on entry into force. For most exports to the United States, immediate tariff elimination, and a transition period of three to ten years for others.

(Continued)

Table 3. (*Continued*)

Agreement/Sector	ANZSCEP	JSEPA	ESFTA	SAFTA	USSFTA
Services	Based on a positive list and to be reviewed with the goal of free trade in services by 2010. Preferential treatment extended to non-parties engaged in "substantive business operations" in either of the parties. Singapore's commitments beyond GATS include professional, telecommunications, financial, business, and transport services.	Based on a positive list; preferential treatment also extended to non-parties engaged in "substantive business operations" in either of the parties. Singapore's commitments beyond GATS include professional, telecommunication, financial, business, and transport services.	Based on a positive list and to be reviewed with the goal of eliminating substantially all remaining restrictions in services covered at the end of ten years. Singapore's commitments beyond GATS include professional, telecommunication, financial, business, and transport services.	Based on a negative list; exceptions to market access and national treatment listed in annexes. Preferential treatment extended to non-parties engaged in "substantive business operations" in either of the parties. Singapore's commitments beyond GATS include professional, telecommunication, financial, business, and transport services.	Based on a negative list, with exceptions to market access and national treatment listed in annexes. Singapore's commitments beyond the GATS include professional, telecommunications, financial, business, and transport services.
Contingency measures	No right to take safeguard measures against each others' imports; anti-dumping provisions are stricter than those applied under GATT Article VI.	May take emergency measures against each others' imports only during the 10-year transition period; anti-dumping measures to be in accordance with GATT Article VI.	May take emergency measures against each others' imports but not anti-dumping measures.	No right to take safeguard measures against each others' imports; anti-dumping rules are stricter than those applied under GATT Article VI.	Safeguard measures may be taken during the ten-year transition period; anti-dumping measures may be taken in accordance with GATT Article VI.

(*Continued*)

Table 3. (*Continued*)

Agreement/ Sector	ANZSCEP	JSEPA	ESFTA	SAFTA	USSFTA
Intellectual property rights	WTO TRIPS Agreement provisions to apply.	WTO TRIPS Agreement provisions to apply. Cooperation on IPR matters, including through a Joint Committee.	WTO TRIPS Agreement provisions to apply.	WTO TRIPS Agreement provisions to apply. Cooperation *inter alia* on enforcement and education.	Singapore to accede to international conventions including WIPO Copyright Treaty, WIPO Performances and Phonographs Treaty, and UPOV. TRIPS-plus provisions include extending copyright protection to life of author plus 70 years, measures against the circumvention of technologies that protect copyright works, protection of well-known marks, extension for unreasonable curtailment of patent term for pharmaceutical products due to delays in marketing approval process.

(*Continued*)

Table 3. (*Continued*)

Agreement/ Sector	ANZSCEP	JSEPA	ESFTA	SAFTA	USSFTA
Competition	Commitment to creating and maintaining open and competitive markets; endeavouring to implement the APEC Principles to Enhance Competition and Regulatory reform. Parties also agreed to consult with each other in the development of any new competition measures.	Cooperation on controlling anti-competitive practices including the exchange of information on such practices.	Cooperation through consultations on eliminating anti-competitive business practices.	Commitment to promote competition by addressing anti-competitive practices including through consultation and review. Within six months of a generic competition law being enacted by Singapore, a review of the competition provisions of the FTA to be conducted.	Commits Singapore to enacting generic competition legislation by 2005 and ensuring that GLCs do not engage in agreements that restrain competition or in exclusionary practices that substantially lessen competition.

(*Continued*)

Table 3. (*Continued*)

Agreement/ Sector	ANZSCEP	JSEPA	ESFTA	SAFTA	USSFTA
Investment	Provisions apply to all goods and those services listed in the parties' schedules.	Provisions apply to all goods and those services listed in the parties' schedules. Performance requirements are prohibited.	Provisions on investment do not apply to measures affecting trade in services and to investors investing in services (subject to a review after ten years).	Provisions apply to all goods and services (except where reservations have been listed by the parties).	Negative list for goods and services except those scheduled, and detailed investor-state dispute settlement provisions. Performance requirements are prohibited.
Government procurement	Single market between the two parties for procurement valued at over SDR 50,000.	Provisions of the WTO GPA apply. Procurement threshold of SDR 100,000.	Provisions of the WTO GPA apply.	Single market between the two parties.	Preferences up to S$102,710 for goods and services for Ministries (S$910,000 for statutory boards), and S$11,376,000 for construction services.
Others					Provisions on labor and environment.

Note: Details of rules of origin under these agreements are provided in Chapter III (Table III.3).
ANZSCEP: New Zealand–Singapore Free Trade Agreement
JSEPA: Japan–Singapore Free Trade Agreement
ESFTA: European Union Free Trade Agreement
SAFTA: Singapore–Australia Free Trade Agreement
USSFTA: United States–Singapore Free Trade Agreement
CECA: India–Singapore Comprehensive Economic Cooperation Agreement
Source: WTO Secretariat, based on the texts of Singapore's bilateral FTAs. Ministry of Trade and Industry, Singapore: http://app.fta.gov.sg/

regarding copyrights and marks (e.g. Madrid Protocol on 31 October 2000, Patent Cooperation Treaty, Trademark Law Treaty, UPOV convention in 1991, WIPO Copyright in 1991 and 1996, and Phonograms Treaty in 1996) that are due to be effective by the beginning of 2005. Overall, bilateral FTAs are creating greater access to local markets and also helping to harmonize the domestic regulatory framework across countries.

Chapter 6

Growing Economic Relations with India: A Case-study in Deepening Integration between South Asia and East Asia

6.1. *De facto* Integration[8]

As noted, Singapore's policy makers have long been cognizant that the small size of the city-state will limit the rate of growth of its domestic Gross Domestic Product (GDP). Accordingly, since the late 1980s, the policy makers have made a conscious decision to invest aggressively overseas, both in order to develop linkages and business opportunities for domestic companies, as well as to make profits abroad (some of which will presumably be repatriated back to Singapore), hence increasing the country's Gross National Product (GNP). Given India's needs for massive financial resources for development, on the one hand, and Singapore's desire to expand its external wing, on the other, one would have expected significant synergies between the two countries. This is particularly so in view of the close geographical proximity between the two countries (particularly South India and Singapore). However, it was only since the mid 1990s as Singapore's political links with India improved

---

[8]This section is informed by Asher and Sen (2005).

under the then Prime Minister Goh Chok Tong that Singapore started viewing India as a serious investment destination. Unlike Japan and Korea, Singapore-owned companies are by and large not major manufacturing powerhouses. Nonetheless, Singapore companies have significant financial resources and expertise in infrastructural development such as townships, industrial parks, real estate and urban planning, airports, seaports, etc.

More generally, Singapore is particularly strong in the logistics sector, an area of comparative weakness for India. However, there are many collaborative ventures between Singapore and various states in India. For instance, the Port of Singapore Authority (PSA) has been involved in the development and management of the Tuticorin Port in Tamil Nadu and the Pipavav port in Gujarat, while Singapore's initial large-scale investment was in the multi-million dollar IT Park in Bangalore in 1994 (by Singapore-based Ascendas). Singapore's investments in India encompass infrastructure, banking, pharmaceuticals, and telecommunication. The Singapore government's holding company, Government of Singapore Investment Corporation (GIC), has emerged as a major Foreign Institutional Investor (FII) in India, thus providing a grater deal of equity capital to many Indian businesses.

Conversely, many Indian companies are increasingly viewing Singapore as a good secondary base to maintain some of their operations to service overseas clients (in the event that services out of India are disrupted for some reason such as conflicts or natural disasters). Singapore is also seen as a good base from which Indian companies can service regional clients. Many Indian companies such as Satyam, Tata Consultancy Services, eSys, VSNL, Bilcare have already established key regional operations in Singapore, and many more are likely to do so in the near future.

While Indian companies are finding it difficult to gain outsourcing contracts from Japanese and Korean firms because of the language and cultural differences as well as a general reluctance of Japanese and Korean firms to partake in offshoring despite the costs savings to be had, there is a belief that Singapore-owned and Singapore-based companies may be more willing and able to outsource in a large way to India.[9] At a strategic and political level, as noted, Singapore has been instrumental in helping India become more accepted into the broader East Asian community of nations. Aggregate trade between India and Singapore has been steadily growing since 1999 and has reached $5 billion in 2003 but has since doubled in 2005 (Tables 1, 2 and 3). Specifically, over the last half-decade, India's imports from Singapore have increased by 27%; during the same period India's exports to Singapore have increased by 100%.[10] In fact in recent years, Singapore's trade with India has outpaced its growth with other Asian neighbors (Figure 1).

6.2. *De jure* Integration: The Comprehensive Economic Co-operation Agreement

The growing closeness in ties between India and the city state is apparent from the establishment of a bilateral Comprehensive Economic Co-operation Agreement (CECA) on 29 June 2005. The Agreement came into force from 1 August 2005. The CECA is an

Table 1. India's Bilateral Trade with Singapore, (US$ billion), 1999–2003

Year	India's exports to Singapore	India's imports from Singapore	India's imports from Singapore less entrepot trade	Total bilateral trade
1999	0.74	2.50	0.61	3.23
2000	1.06	2.74	0.48	3.81
2001	1.13	2.76	0.50	3.90
2002	1.18	2.67	0.40	3.85
2003	1.48	3.16	0.22	4.64

Source: http://www.ficci.com/FICCI/INTERNATIONAL/COUNTRIES/singapore/singapore-commercialrelations.htm

---

[9]Thus far, many of these companies have preferred outsourcing to other ASEAN countries (Philippines or Malaysia) or chosen to automate many frontline services.
[10]It warrants noting that Singapore's exports to India consist of re-exports which constitutes slightly over 50% of Singapore's exports to India.

Table 2. Major Products in Singapore's Domestic Exports to India, 2005

Rank	Product code	Product description	Value (S$ million)	Share in total (%)
1	334	Petroleum Products Refined	1,054	22.3
2	759	Parts For Office & Dp Machines	671	14.2
3	752	Data Processing Machines	478	10.1
4	511	Hydrocarbons Nes	477	10.1
5	892	Printed Matter	220	4.6
6	513	Carboxylic Acids & Deriv	151	3.2
7	776	Electronic Valves	124	2.6
8	898	Musical Instrument & Parts	124	2.6
9	764	Telecommunications Equipment	111	2.4
10	723	Civil Engineering Equipment Parts	84	1.8
		Others	1,231	26.0
		Grand Total	4,726	100.0

Source: Singapore Trade Statistics CD-ROM 2006.

Table 3. Major Products in Singapore's Imports from India, 2005

Rank	Product code	Product description	Value (S$ million)	Share in total (%)
1	667	Precious Stone & Pearl	2,738	40.3
2	334	Petroleum Products Refined	1,802	26.5
3	684	Aluminium	247	3.6
4	897	Jewellery Etc	180	2.7
5	511	Hydrocarbons Nes	130	1.9
6	277	Natural Abrasives	58	0.8
7	542	Medicaments	54	0.8
8	845	Apparel Articles of Textile	47	0.7
9	759	Parts for Office & Dp Machines	47	0.7
10	682	Copper	47	0.7
		Others	1,437	21.2
		Grand Total	6,788	100.0

Source: Singapore Trade Statistics CD-ROM 2006.

integrated package comprising a Free Trade Agreement (FTA), a bilateral agreement on investment, an improved double taxation avoidance agreement, and a cooperation pact in areas like education, science, air services, media, e-commerce, intellectual property and flow of human resources (Table 4).

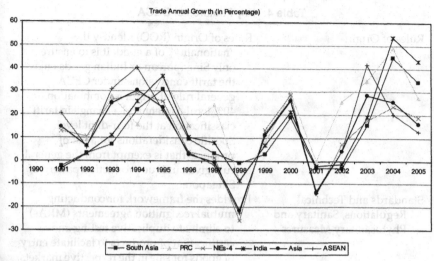

Source: ADB.

Fig. 1. Singapore's Trade Growth with Asian Economies, 1990–2005.

The Agreement aims to catalyze the growing flows of trade, investment and people and intends to develop a long-term economic and strategic partnership between the two countries. Some salient features of the CECA are in order. First, both countries have offered tariff concessions on a number of products. Given Singapore's essentially zero external tariffs, the bulk of the adjustment has fallen on India.[11] India's tariff concessions on goods fall into three main categories.

(a) 506 products have been identified in the early harvest list and are free of duties from 1 August 2005. Products in this list include electronics, instrumentation, pharmaceutical and publishing industries.
(b) A phased elimination list is in place for 4,609 products, and their duties will be gradually phased out by April 1, 2009.[12]

---

[11]Singapore has negligible tariffs on all but six items and it has agreed to bind all its tariff lines at zero customs duty.
[12]Half of the products on this list will be on a fast track scheme whereby their tariffs will be halved quickly.

Table 4. Key Features of CECA

Rules of Origin	Rules of Origin (ROO) identify the "nationality" of a good. It is to ensure only Singaporean or Indian goods enjoy the tariff concessions under CECA. The general rule of origin is combination of 40% local content and a change in tariff classification at the four-digit level. Specific considerations for a list of products that is exempt from the general rule given unique production pattern of Singapore.
Standards and Technical Regulations, Sanitary and Phytosanitary Measures	Provides the framework for conducting mutual recognition agreements (MRAs) to eliminate duplicative testing and certification of products to facilitate entry of goods for sale in the respective markets. Key sectors that are included in this framework are electrical and electronics and telecommunication equipments.
Services Sectors	Both countries have committed to liberalize various services sectors beyond the WTO commitments. Preferential access are given to business services, construction and related engineering services, financial services, telecommunication services, environmental services, tourism and transport services. Financial services: Singapore owned or controlled financial institutions have given greater access to the Indian market (DBS, UOB and OCBC). They are allowed to set up branches and given a quota of 15 branches over 4 years. Indian banks that satisfy Singapore's admission criteria will be given Wholesale bank licenses and up to three bank licenses with Qualifying Full Banks privileges. Asset management: Mutual funds and collective investment schemes (CIS) could be listed in Stock Exchange by registered fund managers in the respective countries.

(Continued)

Table 4. *(Continued)*

	Telecommunication services: India will increase its limit from 25% to 49% for basic, cellular and long-distance services and 74% for internet and infrastructure services. Singapore companies will be given access to public infrastructure to offer their services. E-Commerce: Commitment to promote a liberalized environment for electronic commerce.
Movement of Natural Persons	Easier access for movement of natural persons. Intra-corporate transferees (i.e. managers, executives, and specialist within organizations) will be permitted to stay and work in India and Singapore for an initial period of up to two years or the period of the contract, whichever is less. The period could be extended up to three years and total term not exceeding eight years.
Education	University linkages: NUS-IIT-B tie-up

Source: Ministry of Trade and Industry, Singapore: http://app.fta.gov.sg/

(c) Some 6,551 products are in a negative list, meaning that they will not be liberalized and will continue to receive the Most Favored Nation (MFN) rates on their imports. The concessions given by India cover about 80% of Singapore's present exports to India.

The major items of India's exports to Singapore in 2003 included crude petroleum, refined motor spirit, petroleum oils, polished diamonds for jewellery, polished industrial diamonds, articles of jewellery, aluminium unwrought, aluminium sheets, parts & accessories of computers, textiles and fabrics, dyes, acids, insecticides, fungicides, household articles of stainless steel, metals, medical equipments, food items, valves/taps cocks for pipes, boilers, tanks etc, bus/lorry tyres and tobacco. These items have constituted over 70% of India's exports to Singapore in value terms. The major items of India's imports from Singapore in 2003 were parts and accessories of computers and computer peripherals, integrated circuits, cellular phones, CD Roms, chemicals, parts of boring and sinking machinery, metals, sewing machines, ball/roller bearings, parts and equipment, medical instruments and appliances and cigarettes. These items have constituted over 60% of India's imports from Singapore in value terms.[13] The CECA is expected to enhance bilateral trade in these set of products while also opening up further areas of trade between the two countries.

Given the importance of the services sector to both India and Singapore, the CECA has also focussed on the removal of quantitative restrictions (and guaranteeing market access) on many professional services, education, distribution, financial, transportation, telecommunication, environmental, tourism, construction and related engineering services. Most notable is the agreement on financial services, whereby, as part of the pact, India has agreed to allow three Singapore banks to set up wholly owned subsidiaries in the country subject to meeting the Reserve Bank of India's (RBI) prudential norms. Singapore's three main local banks, viz. DBS, OCBC and UOB, are to be offered national treatment on par with Indian banks when it comes to branching, operating venues, and prudential requirements. The Singapore banks have also been permitted to acquire private Indian banks under the existing foreign investment policy framework, though they will have to comply with the overall restrictions imposed on foreign banks, and they cannot exceed 15% of total banking sector assets. Conversely, Indian banks and financial institutions have been granted preferential access into the Singapore market. Indian banks that satisfy Singapore's admission criteria will be given Wholesale Bank licences and up to three bank licences with Qualifying Full Banks (QFBs) privileges. This allows the Indian banks in Singapore to undertake electronic fund transfer and establishing ATMs and clearances. In addition, India insurers and capital market intermediaries will have open access to set up in Singapore.

Another notable aspect of the CECA pertains to the movement of Natural Persons (Mode 4). Specifically, both countries are to ease restrictions for temporary entry under four categories of

---

[13]See http://www.ficci.com/FICCI/INTERNATIONAL/COUNTRIES/singapore/singapore-commercialrelations.htm

persons — business visitors, short-term service suppliers, professionals and intra-corporate transferees. As elaborated upon by Das and Sen (2005):

(B)business visitors with five-year multiple journey visa will be permitted to enter and engage in business activities for a period of up to two months (which may be extended up to one month), while intra-corporate transferees (managers, executives and specialists within organizations) will be permitted to stay and work in India and Singapore for an initial period of up to two years or the period of the contract, whichever is less. Further, short-term service suppliers will be granted temporary entry to service their contracts for an initial period of up to 90 days and professionals employed in 127 specific occupations will be allowed entry and stay for up to one year or the duration of contract, whichever is less. This benefit is extended to both citizens and permanent residents of the two parties and is not subjected to any pre-conditions, such as labor market testing or economic needs test. However, market access for these professionals in either India or Singapore is subject to negotiations on bilateral recognition of qualifications, which are expected to be complete in next one year.[14]

Given that Singapore accounts for almost half of India's trade with ASEAN, and the CECA is the first comprehensive agreement that India has signed, it is understandable that the agreement is viewed in some quarters as a sort of pathfinder or template for India with the rest of its East Asian neighbors. Particular attention has been focussed on India's willingness to liberalize its financial sector. However, an important caveat should be kept in mind with regard to this sectoral liberalization. Concerns have been expressed in some quarters that India has not been able to obtain maximum reciprocal benefits from the agreement. Specifically, while Singapore has three main local banks that have all been given access to the large Indian market and Singapore has reciprocated by extending full licenses to three Indian banks, Singapore offered unlimited access to all US banks to Singapore. Table 5 summarizes the commitments Singapore

---

[14]Other issues relating to customs procedures, rules of origin (ROOs), mutual recognition agreements (MRAs) on standards and technical regulations, sanitary and phytosanitary measures, dispute settlement procedures, e-commerce, IPR protection, double-taxation, and separate pacts in various sub-sectors including air services, e-commerce have also been negotiated as part of the CECA.

Table 5. Singapore's Financial Sector Commitments to India vs. the US

Type of service	Commitments to US	Commitments to India
Qualified Full Banking	No restriction and free access to locations.	Restricted to three.
Insurance–Life and Non-Life	Free presence with national treatment.	Commercial presence under Mode 3 (i.e. need to establish branches).
Forex Dealings	No approval needed.	Require prior approval from local authorities.
Investment Advisory	National treatment for cross-border services.	Curbs under Modes 1, 2, 3.
Insurance Brokers	Mode 3 presence not required.	Placed under Mode 3 with commercial presence.

Note: Directors of Singapore-based Indian banks must be Singapore citizens or permanent residents.
Source: Srinath (2005).

has offered to the US compared to those offered to India. There is pressure on the government to ensure that, at the minimum, in future trade agreements India receives the same level of concessions offered to others.[15] This apart, given the limited agricultural sector in Singapore, this issue has not been a point of contention; however it could become a problem if India negotiates agreements with other East Asian countries which protect their agricultural sector such as Japan. Nonetheless, from Singapore's perspective, the CECA not only promotes trade in services and investment across the two countries, it also allows for certain deregulation of the Indian economy, it commits India to open and liberal trade policy with Singapore and thereby "locking-in" to similar treatments to future bilateral negotiations with other ASEAN countries.

---

[15]This said, it is probably unfair to focus on a single issue, but the important issue in such agreements is the idea of issue-linkage. For instance, India may have received somewhat less favorable terms on the financial services side but it has received concessions desired on cross-border labor mobility.

Chapter 7

Policy Implications

Singapore is among the most open and pro-business economies in the world. It is renowned for its political stability, clean government, efficient systems and world class infrastructure, including telecommunication networks. The focus of attention of policy makers in the country has always been on how to take steps to facilitate the city state's economic integration with the rest of the world as opposed to any specific region or subregion.

Singapore policy makers have actively promoted cross-border investment, removed almost all barriers to trade, removing other frictions to trade by promoting efficiency in cross-border flow of goods, services and selected labor flows (via paperless trading and removed most visa restrictions for short-term business and leisure travellers and promoting transparency and certainty in regulations and procedures). Singapore has also actively participated in regional and international trade and investment fora (including ASEAN, APEC, WTO, etc) and has simultaneously been vigorously seeking out bilateral trade pacts with many countries around the world so as to network the country as much as possible with the global economy.

In a lot of ways Singapore can be seen as best practice in the area of international trade and investment promotion and facilitation. This said, there are some challenges for the city-state going forward.

One, it is commonly noted that since Singapore has one of the most liberal trade and investment regimes in the world with near zero tariff rates on most goods (and limited non-tariff barriers), the

77

scope for trade diversion (i.e. replacement of lower cost suppliers from non-member countries) from Singapore's vantage point is quite small. Nonetheless, it would be wrong to conclude that there are no ill effects whatsoever. An important issue of concern is to what extent the various bilateral, subregional and transnational arrangements might contradict each other, and if and how such contradictions will be overcome. Only time will tell. However, given the proliferation of a number of overlapping trade agreements raises many technical problems with regard to the implementation of special provisions or rules of origin (ROOs) which are meant to prevent goods being re-exported from/circumvented through the lower tariff country to the higher tariff one (i.e. *trade deflection*).

Even with a single FTA, a concern is that ROOs with a particular country, say the US, may be sufficiently prohibitive so as to induce Singapore exporters to source their inputs from the US than some other developing country in Asia (such as Korea, for instance). In other words, the US exports its external tariffs to Singapore. ROOs also give rise to significant costs due to the need for administrative surveillance and implementation. In practice, ROOs are particularly complex as they have to take into account tariffs on imported intermediate goods used in products produced within the FTA. The book-keeping and related costs escalate sharply as production gets more integrated internationally (what Jagdish Bhagwati has colorfully termed the *"spaghetti bowl"* phenomenon; see Baldwin, 2006) and countries get involved with an increasing number of separate but overlapping FTAs. For instance, under the ASEAN regional agreement, imported products must be wholly produced in an ASEAN country or must have at least a cumulative basis of 40% of the finished product with ASEAN content. In the US–Singapore FTA, products must be wholly produced in United States, or for electronic products produced by Singaproean or US value-added content ranging from 30% to 60% of the f.o.b. price of the final product. For certain chemical or petroluem products a specificed production process must have occurred in the United States or Singapore to be considered for different tariff classification of the final product (see Table 1 for full details).

Table 1. Singapore's Approach to Implementation of WTO Obligations (inc ROOs)

Section	Current status of WTO obligations implementation
WTO Agreement, Annex 1A (Goods)	Singapore has already implemented our UR tariff binding commitments, which is to bind 70% of tariff lines at rates of 10% and below by 1 January 1996.
	Singapore has brought its anti-dumping act (1996) and regulations (1997) into conformity with the WTO Agreement on Implementation of Article VI of GATT and fulfilled the various notification requirements under the Agreement.
	Singapore has brought its countervailing duty act (1996) and regulations (1997) into conformity with the WTO Agreement on Subsidies and Countervailing Measures. Singapore has also phased out its export subsidies or brought them into conformity with the Agreement by 1999, three years ahead of the committed time frame.
	Singapore maintains stringent standards on agricultural and food safety while recognizing foreign national standards and testing carried out by competent foreign authorities in accordance with internationally accepted protocols.
	Singapore has already implemented the WTO Customs Valuation Agreement for assessing customs duty on imported goods on 17 October 1997. Singapore's Customs (Valuation) (Import Duty) Regulations conform to this Agreement.
	Singapore does not maintain any TRIMS that do not conform with the Agreement on Trade-Related Investment Measures.
WTO Agreement, Annex 1B (Services)	Singapore has implemented its commitments under the GATS Agreement.
WTO Agreement, Annex 1C (IPR)	Singapore has implemented TRIPS on 1 January 1999, a year ahead of schedule.
WTO Plurilateral	Singapore was one of the signatories to the WTO Ministerial Declaration on Trade in Information Technology.
Agreements	Products, which was agreed at the close of the first WTO Ministerial Conference on 13 December 1996 in Singapore. ITA is to be implemented over four stages from 1997 to 2000. Singapore has implemented our ITA tariff binding commitments, in which all bindings are at zero rates of duty.

(Continued)

Table 1. (*Continued*)

Section	Current status of WTO obligations implementation
Rules of Origin	Singapore's rules of origin are simple and liberal and comply with the above disciplines. We have notified our existing rules of origin to the WTO.
	Essentially, there are no rules of origin specifically applied to normal imports into Singapore. There are rules of origin applicable to imports entering Singapore under the ASEAN preferential tariff schemes. For normal exports to qualify as of Singapore origin, it must either:
	(a) be wholly obtained in Singapore or
	(b) possess a local content of at least 25% of the ex-factory price of the product if it is manufactured with imported materials. Products which undergo minimal processing are not conferred originating status.
	Applications for the Singapore Certificate of Origin (COO) can be made through Singapore Customs (http://www.tradenet.gov.sg) and six authorized organizations.
	Singapore has been actively participating in the harmonization work programme being conducted under WTO/WCO.

Source: http://www.apec-iap.org

Concerted efforts must be taken by the policymakers to harmonize its ROOs in the various trade pacts it has signed and will continue to sign in the future. Given that the city state has been at the forefront of the FTA phenomenon, it is incumbent on its policy makers to play a more pro-active role in helping to establish a set of multilateral ROO and try to see through its global acceptance and implementation.

Two, although both manufacturing and services sector are "twin-engines" of growth for the economy, increasingly, it is observed that the services sector will play an important role in output and employment creation in the economy. As noted, several key factors are already in place for improving the efficiency and productive performance of the economy. Further improvements in and the successful implementation of the competition policy could provide strong improvements in efficiency from greater competition from more open economic activities. Particular attention needs to be paid to the further restructuring and liberalization of various infrastructure-related services including the telecommunications sector, the energy and gas industry and the finance industry. In this respect, the future role of GLCs in the economic and global integration must be clearly defined in terms of their role in the role in the economy and greater corporate transparency. The introduction of the competition law that will apply to all commercial and economic activities of private and GLCs is important in ensuring efficient markets and hence greater transparency in competition in the economy.

Three, given that Singapore has taken a strong position in the WTO-plus bilateral FTAs, the full benefits of such an undertaking can only be attained if ASEAN see the potential benefits of the WTO-plus bilateral FTAs in services sector. Since the services sector will be crucial for the next phase of growth, a common framework for cohesive and coordinated ASEAN to engage bilateral agreements with major trading partners should be developed. Within ASEAN, focus should be on enhancing the pace of integration of some sectors like tourism and air transport. Singapore can lead the way in this regard given its comparative advantage in many services and its experience thus far with services liberalization. However, the gap in liberalization of the services sector among the ASEAN countries tends to be quite diverse and incoherent. Many other ASEAN countries have tended to take a more protectionist in the post-Asian crisis liberalization of the services sector, and thereby adopting a defensive and cautious approach. In particular, ASEAN countries should be more pro-active in negotiating on key sensitive sectors to reduce barriers for trade in services.

In fact, the signing of FTAs by Singapore appears to have energized other ASEAN countries to adopt more proactive trade policies and raised the urgency to pursue more liberal trade and investment policies. The response from ASEAN, especially Malaysia and Thailand, have been to seek their own FTAs to match the record number of FTAs signed by Singapore. The focus on creating trade has also revitalized the regional economies to promote deeper integration through ASEAN. In 2006, the ASEAN Secretariat announced that ASEAN member countries are well on their way towards AFTA with tariff elimination in ASEAN-6 and Cambodia, Lao, PDR, Myanmar and Vietnam, bringing down the tariff rates to the 0–5% range. The current emphasis of AFTA is on trade facilitation, liberalization of services, and opening up of the investment regimes in ASEAN.

Four, even more emphasis needs to be placed on intellectual property rights (IPR) protection. For instance, the adoption and recognition of global standards on IPRs will have significant impact on innovation and greater spillovers from foreign direct investments in the Singapore economy.

Five, while the Singapore International Arbitration Center has entered into a joint venture with the American Arbitration Association to open a new arbitration center in Singapore — the International Center for Dispute Resolution Singapore, further efforts are needed to ensure a develop a more sophisticated and integrated dispute resolution complex to facilitate business transaction in the city-state.

Six, the industrial strategy for moving to higher value-added activities has, until recently, focused on multinational activities and GLCs to move the economy into key industries. In this process, small and medium-sized enterprises (SMEs) are critically marginalized and "crowded-out" of the industrial development. The development of SMEs will be crucial for the next phase of growth for the Singapore economy and to reap the full-potential benefits of the FTAs through linkages and spillovers from open industrial activities. With the disinvestment of government linked corporations (GLCs) and with the introduction of the competition policy noted previously, there should be greater scope for SMEs to compete in markets that have so far been dominated by GLCs. This ought to create greater entrepreneurial activities within the domestic economy. It bears keeping in mind that in a knowledge-based economy, entrepreneurship will be very crucial for a dynamic and innovative economy.

Seven, another important area of development is in human capital. In the new global economy, the quality of human resources is key to success. Given that 34% of domestic labor force still only has below secondary education, it is imperative that the workforce should be retrained and upgraded for the new growth areas in both the manufacturing and services sector. The aim of the Workers Development Agency (WDA) is to enhance the productivity and employability of the workers through training, retraining, and retaining workers in the labor market. Global talent can continue to help supplement human capital needs of the economy. Greater flexibility in the institutions to ensure rapid and flexible response to external shocks and imbalances will be very crucial for the small-open economy. The Singapore government embarked on a flexible labor market policy and introduced wage reform recently. This is to ensure greater flexibility and competitiveness in the wage system in the Singapore economy.

Eight, given the importance of foreign labor to supplement domestic labor and the continued dependence on business and tourism flows, continued efforts need to be placed on ensuring hassle-free immigration and customs procedures. Mutual recognition of foreign degrees, especially from selected institutes in South Asia can facilitate the city state's desire to remain attractive to global talent.

Nine, apart from a need to further strengthening of the anti-competitive agreements, decisions and practices noted above, there is a need to ensure greater transparency in government tendering procedures so as to ensure openness, fairness and efficiency in business operations and procedures.[16]

Ten, given Singapore's geographical location, its multicultural environment, its economic openness, as well as the fact that it is a hub for trade, logistics and IT and business and financial services,

---

[16] "GeBIZ" is Singapore's one stop e-procurement system where those interested can find all procurement opportunities. Potential suppliers can register as a GeBIZ Trading Partner.

Singapore is uniquely placed to facilitate greater engagement between South and East Asia. Indeed, Singapore has played an important complementary role to India's "Look East" policy, hence facilitating India's integration fairly rapidly with the rest of East Asia. Singapore should continue to work towards integrating South and East Asia more closely via actively promoting the East Asian Summit (EAS) and promoting more open membership of APEC to include India and other South Asian economies. The city state should also consider expanding its FTAs to include more South Asian economies in addition to India through bilateral pacts and/or three-way agreements. Given Singapore's strengths in logistics, including development of industrial parks and townships, Singapore can, along with Japan and Korea, play a major role in the industrial development of India and the rest of South Asia and in turn help the Indian subcontinent to integrate even more closely with the rest of East Asia.

Annex 1

Singapore's Approach to Investment in 2004

Section	Current investment measures applied
General Policy Framework	Singapore is committed to achieving a free and open investment regime and actively promotes foreign investment. The Economic Development Board (EDB), the agency that focuses on investment promotion, helps to provide information pertaining to investment. The policy framework is that businesses in Singapore need to register with the Accounting and Corporate Regulatory Authority, the previous Registry of Companies and Businesses now merged with the Public Accountants Board.
	With exceptions for national security purposes and in certain industries, no restrictions are placed on foreign ownership of Singapore operations. Applicable to both foreign and local investors, only a few specific products require government approval for manufacture under the Control of Manufacture Act (COMA). To-date, these are beer and stout, cigars, drawn steel products, cigarettes, matches, chewing gum other than medicinal gum and oral dental gum.
	To improve the protection of intellectual property rights and enhance the regulatory system for the manufacture of optical discs, the manufacture of optical disks is now legislated under the Manufacture of Optical Discs Act (MODA). A licence is required for the manufacture of optical discs under the Manufacture of Optical Discs Act (MODA) with effect from July 2004. CDs (compact disc), CD-ROMs (compact disc-read only memory), VCDs (video compact disc), DVDs (digital video disc) and

(Continued)

85

Section	Current investment measures applied
	DVD-ROMs (digital video disc–read only memory), as well as master discs and stampers used in the production of optical discs are no longer regulated under the COMA but under the MODA. Laws, regulations, administrative guidelines and policies are in place and continue to be improved. If there are changes, public announcements are made and ample timeframe is provided for implementation.
	To enable a framework conducive to business growth and bilateral investments, Singapore has FTAs with ASEAN, New Zealand, Japan, the European Free Trade Association, Australia, the United States and Jordan.
Transparency	Singapore has a regulatory investment environment based on clarity, fair competition and sound business practice. There are minimal investment regulations. The APEC Leaders' Transparency Standards on Investment apply, as described below:
	1. Singapore's investment laws, regulations, procedures and administrative rulings of general application ("investment measures") are promptly published or made available online to enable interested persons and other economies to become acquainted with them. Investment measures apply to all investors irrespective of nationality.
	2. The Singapore government promotes feedback and consultation with relevant bodies and the public. The government publishes in advance any investment measures proposed for adoption and provides a reasonable opportunity for public comment. There is a government online consultation portal where public agencies post consultation papers to seek feedback and ideas.
	3. Upon request from an interested person or another economy, the Singapore government endeavors to promptly provide information and respond to questions pertaining to any actual or proposed investment measures. Suitable contact points including the Economic Development Board are in place to facilitate communications with the requesting party.

(Continued)

Section	Current investment measures applied

4. Singapore has in place appropriate domestic procedures to enable prompt review and correction of final administrative actions, other than those taken for sensitive prudential reasons, regarding investment matters covered by the transparency standards. The system provides:

   (a) for tribunals or panels that are impartial and independent of any office or authority entrusted with administrative enforcement and have no substantial interest in the outcome of the investment matter;
   (b) parties to any proceeding with a reasonable opportunity to present their respective positions;
   (c) parties to any proceeding with a decision based on the evidence and submissions of record or, where required by domestic law, the record complied by the administrative authority; and
   (d) assurance subject to appeal or further review under domestic law, that such decisions will be implemented by, and govern the practice of, the offices or authorities regarding the administrative action at issue.

5. There is no need for screening, evaluation or scoring of projects for their approval in Singapore. The Control of Manufacture Act sets out the list of products that require approval and registration for manufacture. The list is applicable to all investors irrespective of nationality.

6. The procedures for business registration of investment which is necessary and government licensing of investment if required under specific sectors are kept clear and simple. Explanation of steps regarding application and registration and criteria for license including information on standards, technical regulations and conformity requirements are published and made available online in Singapore. A central online business license service has started operating and will be further developed.

7. No prior authorization of investment is required in Singapore and hence no procedures for the purpose exist. The government has reviewed the procedures

(Continued)

(Continued)

Section	Current investment measures applied
	for business registration and licence application to ensure that they are simple and transparent.
	8. Singapore through the Economic Development Board makes available to investors all rules and other appropriate information relating to investment promotion programmes. These are also published under the Economic Expansion Incentives (Relief from Income Tax) Act available online.
	9. Free trade agreements negotiated contain investor/state dispute settlement mechanism and transparency provisions.
	10. Singapore participates fully in APEC-wide efforts to update the APEC Investment Guidebook.
Non-discrimination	Singapore provides MFN treatment. All foreign investors alike are allowed to maintain 100% foreign equity and are free to make their own decisions on markets, technology licensing and other investment areas. The Government actively encourages foreign investment and generally treats foreign capital the same as local capital. Generally there is no restriction on the types of businesses that may be set up in Singapore, and there are no limitations on foreign companies' access to sources of finance. Singapore extends national treatment economy-wide.
Expropriation and Compensation	The provision for expropriation and compensation is usually included in bilateral investment guarantee agreements. There has been no instance of disputes brought to court for expropriation and compensation of foreign investment in Singapore.
Protection from Strife and Similar Events	Singapore has bilateral investment guarantee agreements (IGAs) with other economies to promote and protect investment coming into and going out of Singapore. In general, under the agreements, investments by nationals or companies of both contracting parties in each other's economy are protected for an initial period of usually 15 years against war and non-commercial risks like expropriation and nationalization. In the event of non-commercial risks, Singapore will compensate such foreign investors in a manner no less favorable than that which the latter party accords to investors of any third economy. There are similar provisions in our FTAs.

(Continued)

(Continued)

Section	Current investment measures applied
	To-date, Singapore has signed IGAs with ASEAN, Bahrain, Bangladesh, Belgo-Luxembourg Economic Union, Belarus, Bulgaria, Cambodia, Canada, China, Czech Republic, Egypt, France, Germany, Hungary, Mauritius, Mongolia, Laos, Latvia, Netherlands, Pakistan, Peru, Poland, Riau Archipelago, Slovenia, Sri Lanka, Switzerland, Taiwan, United Kingdom, United States of America, Vietnam, Uzbekistan and Zimbabwe. Besides bilateral IGAs, the Multilateral Investment Guarantee Agency (MIGA) which Singapore joined in 1998 provides guarantees at the multilateral level against certain non-commercial risks for eligible investors.
Transfers of capital related to investments	There are no restrictions on the repatriation/transfer of profits, capital gains and dividends arising from an investment. The free transfer of funds related to investment is also a provision in bilateral investment guarantee agreements and the investment chapter of FTAs. As part of its globalization strategy, Singapore encourages its companies to invest abroad.
Performance Requirements	There are no laws or policies stating performance requirements, local content requirements or technology transfer requirements which are inconsistent with WTO TRIMs. All contracts are treated as commercial dealings.
Entry and Stay of Personnel	Singapore welcomes foreign talent. Business or social visit passes are required for the temporary entry and sojourn of key foreign technical and managerial personnel for the purpose of engaging in activities connected with foreign investment. Foreign personnel require a work pass to engage in employment. The three tiers of work passes are: (i) P passes for those who hold administrative, professional and managerial jobs, entrepreneurs and investors and specialists; (ii) Q1 passes for skilled workers and technicians; and (iii) S passes for middle-tier skilled workers. Entry visas are required for holders of travel documents issued by the governments of Afghanistan, Algeria, Bangladesh, China, Egypt, Hong Kong (documents of identity) India, Iran, Iraq, Jordan, Lebanon, Libya, Morocco, Myanmar, Commonwealth of Independent States, Pakistan, Saudi Arabia, Somalia, Sudan, Syria, Tunisia and Yemen.

(Continued)

Section	Current investment measures applied
Settlement of Disputes	In its bilateral IGAs and FTAs, Singapore allows for prompt settlement of investment related disputes through consultations and negotiations and, in case of failure, arbitration. Singapore has institutionalized and internationalized arbitration. This has been achieved through ratification of the International Convention on the Settlement of Investment Disputes between States and Nationals of other States and the Convention on the Recognition and Enforcement of Foreign Arbitral Awards or the New York Convention and through the creation of the Singapore International Arbitration Center. Singapore enacted the Arbitration (International Investment Disputes) Act in 1968 to implement the Convention and the International Arbitration Act in 1994 to provide the framework for international arbitration. The latter was based on a model law adopted by the UN General Assembly, namely the United Nations Commission for International Trade Law (UNCITRAL). The New York Convention makes more effective the international recognition of arbitration agreements and foreign arbitral awards and the enforcement of the arbitration award.
Intellectual Property	Singapore's intellectual property rights laws are in line with World Trade Organization requirements. Singapore has been a member of WIPO since 1990. Singapore has its own patent law, the Patents Act 1994 and the Patent Rules 1995 and has acceded to several international IP treaties including the Paris Convention, the Budapest Treaty, the Patent Cooperation Treaty, the Berne Convention, the Nice Agreement and the Madrid Protocol. Accession allows patents and trade marks filed in Singapore to be examined worldwide. Copyright protection is provided under the Copyright Act without the need for registration or application. The Government has provided relatively good protection for intellectual property with enforcement and raids on counterfeit goods stepped up. To improve the protection of intellectual property rights and enhance the regulatory system for the manufacture of optical discs, a licence is required for the manufacture of optical discs under the Manufacture of Optical Discs Act (MODA). CDs (compact disc), CD-ROMs (compact disc-read only

(Continued)

Section	Current investment measures applied
	memory), VCDs (video compact disc), DVDs (digital video disc) and DVD-ROMs (digital video disc-read only memory), as well as master discs and stampers used in the production of optical discs are included in the list.
Avoidance of Double Taxation	Singapore has signed bilateral agreements to avoid double taxation with 52 economies. These are Australia, Austria, Bangladesh, Bahrain, Belgium, Bulgaria, Canada, China, Cyprus, Czech Republic, Denmark, Eqypt, Finland, France, Germany, Hungary, India, Indonesia, Israel, Italy, Japan, Korea, Kuwait, Latvia, Lithuania, Luxembourg, Malaysia, Mauritius, Mexico, Mongolia, Myanmar, Netherlands, New Zealand, Norway, Oman, Pakistan, Papua New Guinea, Philippines, Poland, Portugal, Romania, Russia, South Africa, Sri Lanka, Sweden, Switzerland, Taiwan, Thailand, Turkey, United Arab Emirates, United Kingdom and Vietnam. The agreements generally allow tax credit for the foreign tax paid on the remitted amount up to the amount of Singapore tax payable on the same income.
Competition Policy and Regulatory Reform	There are no antitrust and other laws to regulate competition in Singapore. All industries and services are developed to enhance national competitiveness. There is a process of privatization of Government services to stay ahead of competition. A new competition law is being developed to prevent companies from engaging in anti-competitive behavior. The public has been consulted, and the Competition Bill has been tabled in Parliament. A new statutory board would enforce the competition law.
Business Facilitating Measures to Improve the Domestic Business Environment	Besides quality physical infrastructure including one-stop shop facilities for greater efficiency, legal, financial, accounting, taxation, corporate governance and labor sourcing system capabilities are in place, serving well the domestic business environment and adding to Singapore's attractiveness to investment.
	The Zero-In-Process (ZIP) programme of the Civil Service to provide swifter and more integrated service to the public is in place. The BizFile programme of the Accounting and Corporate Regulatory Authority enables business to set up shop in Singapore with a quicker and cheaper start. The E-government Action Plan I launched in June 2000 resulted in about 1,600 public services provided online

(Continued)

(Continued)

Section	Current investment measures applied
	and in a cost-effective way by July 2003. Arising from the Economic Review Committee's call to minimise government rules and regulations, the work of the Pro-enterprise Panel (a joint public and private sector committee set up in 2000 to promote a more pro-business environment) and the Rules Review Panel resulted in the removal or relaxation of several rules and regulation.
	The International Accounting Standards was adopted as the Singapore Accounting Standard from Jan 2003. All Singapore listed companies (except those with market capitalization of $20 million and below, which were given one-year deferment) have to report financial accounts on a quarterly basis.

Source: http://www.apec-iap.org

Annex 2

Singapore's Current Tariff Arrangements

Section	Current tariff arrangements
Bound Tariffs	Singapore has bound 5,636 (94%) of the total 5,981 tariff lines at rates of 6.5% and below. This excludes the 55 tariff lines for alcohol and tobacco products which have been bound at applied specific rates of duty. This is also based on 2002 HS Nomenclature.
Applied Tariffs	Singapore has fully implemented the tariff elements of the sectoral proposals under the EVSL initiative on the basis of the product coverage and end rates endorsed by Trade Ministers in June 1998.
	Customs and excise duties are only levied on 4 broad categories of goods, namely, intoxicating liquors, tobacco products, motor vehicles and petroleum products. Of the tariff lines in these categories, only four lines of alcoholic products viz. beer, stout, medicated samsoo and other samsoo attract both customs and excise duties. There are 82 other tariff lines that attract excise duty.
	For the complete list of dutiable goods and contact details, please visit http://www.customs.gov.sg.
Tariff Quotas	Singapore does not impose tariff quotas on any products.
Tariff Preferences	Under the ASEAN the Common Effective Preferential Scheme, (http://www.aseansec.org/economic/afta/afta_ag2.htm), with effect from 1 January 2001, Singapore offers duty-free access on all 6,036 tariff lines (HS 9-digit level, 2002) in the "Inclusion List".
	Singapore also offers duty-free access for all 6,036 tariff lines (2002) to the various preferential trade partners.

(Continued)

(Continued)

Section	Current tariff arrangements
Transparency of Tariff Regime	Six chapters, with 16 tariff headings of Singapore's tariff schedule (effective from 1 January 2002), are available for viewing on the APEC Tariff database (http://www.apectariff.org/).

Source: http://www.apec-iap.org

Annex 3

Singapore's Current Non-tariff Measures Applied

Section	Current non-tariff measures applied
Quantitative Import Restrictions/ Prohibitions	— Chewing gum (excluding Oral Dental and Medicinal chewing gums)
	— Cigarette & table lighters in the shape of a pistol or revolver
	— Rough diamonds from Liberia and other non-Kimberley Process participants
	— Round logs and timber products originating in Liberia
	— Fire-crackers
	— Medicines/drugs containing amidopyrine, noramidopyrine, amygdalin, danthron, pangamic acid and suprofen
	— Tobacco products which do not comply with stipulated nicotine and tar limits.
	— Cosmetics containing prohibited substances/additives above the stipulated limits.
	— Confectionery, food product, toy or any article that is designed to resemble a tobacco product or which is sold in a package designed to resemble a tobacco product.
	— Articles of asbestos
	— Used motor vehicles more than three years old
	— Rhinoceros horn (parts and products)
	— Ivory for commercial consignments & tiger products
	— Plants of rubber, cocoa, coconut & palm oil from Central & South America & West & Central Africa
	— Controlled telecommunications equipment such as scanning receivers, military communication equipment & automatic call diverters

(Continued)

95

(*Continued*)

Section	Current non-tariff measures applied
Quantitative Export Restrictions/ Prohibitions	Under the Regulation of Imports and Exports Act, 1996, Singapore prohibits exports of certain products, for example arms and related materials, to certain countries, like Rwanda, Sierra Leone and Iraq. Some of the products prohibited for export include certain ozone-depleting substances, ivory and derivatives of tiger and rhinoceros horn and scheduled chemicals under the CWC.
Import Levies	None
Export Levies	Singapore does not impose any levies on the export of goods.
Discretionary Import Licensing	— Artificial sweetening agents, food containing artificial sweetening agents and irradiated food — Specific plants, plant products and other materials (insects, micro-organisms and soil) — Endangered species — Fruit or jackpot machine — Hazardous substances (poisons) — Radioactive materials and irradiating apparatus — Medicines, poisons, drugs, Chinese proprietary medicines and Category 1 cosmetic products — Controlled telecommunication equipment (other than those specified under the prohibited import list) — Rice — Poppy seeds (kaskas) — Precursor Chemicals — Arms and explosives — Scheduled chemicals under the Chemical Weapons Convention–National Authority (Chemical Weapons Convention)
Automatic Import Licensing	— Fresh fruits and vegetables, plants and plant produce, meat and meat products, animals/birds/eggs/ biologics, veterinary medicaments, animal feed, endangered species, imports, exports or transshipments of fish other than ornamental fish, imports, exports or transshipments of ornamental fish, milk powder — skimmed (colored for animal feed) — Amusement machines, coin or disc-operated, including pin-tables, shooting galleries & cinematography machines

(*Continued*)

(*Continued*)

Section	Current non-tariff measures applied
	— Mastering equipment and replication equipment for CDs, CD-ROMs, VCDs, DVDs and DVD-ROMs — Publications, gramophone records, paintings and prints — Films, video tapes and video discs — Cellulose Nitrates, machetes, axes, SOS shrill alarms, handcuffs, Christmas crackers, articles of clothing intended as protection against attack, including bullet-proof vests; steel helmets, toy guns including pistols and revolvers — Certain ozone-depleting substances (imports for re-exports)
Discretionary Export Licensing	— Arms, ammunition, implements of war & atomic energy materials & equipment — Articles of clothing for protection against attack (i.e. Steel helmets, toy guns and handcuffs) — Controlled drugs (e.g. Morphine, Pethidine and other therapeutic products) under the Single Convention on Narcotics Drugs and psychotropic substances (e.g. diazepam, midozalam and phentermine) under the Convention on Psychotropic Substances — Animals, birds, plants and wildlife under CITES
Voluntary Export Restraints	Under the WTO Agreement on Textiles and Clothing (ATC), Singapore maintains three bilateral export restraints with Canada, the European Union, and the United States.
Export Subsidies	Singapore's DTD Scheme conforms to the WTO Agreement on Subsidies & Countervailing Measures.
Minimum Import Prices	Singapore does not impose any minimum import prices.
Other Non-tariff Measures Maintained	Technical Standards and Requirements — With effect from 1 Jan 2001, all petrol and diesel-driven vehicles, before they can be registered for use in Singapore, are required to comply with the exhaust emission standards as specified in the European Directive: 　(i) 96/69/EC for passenger cars and light duty vehicles with maximum laden weight (MLW) of 3,500 kg or less, and

(*Continued*)

(Continued)

Section	Current non-tariff measures applied
	(ii) 91/542/EEC Stage II for heavy-duty vehicles with MLW of more than 3,500 kg.

— Importers of bottled natural mineral water, drinking and spring water are required to submit to the Food Control Division of the Agri-Food & Veterinary Authority of Singapore an original health certificate issued by the country of origin for every incoming consignment. The document should show the source where the water is obtained and certify that the natural mineral water, drinking or spring water is genuine.

— Importers of soy sauce/oyster sauce, beancurd sheets/sticks, porcelain foodwares, flour/starch, nuts, corn, irradiated food, mineral water, whisky/brandy, preserved fruits and vegetables, agar agar or Eastern Europe foodstuff are required to contact the Food Control Division of the Agri-Food & Veterinary Authority of Singapore or fax the import permit for inspection/sampling.

— Importers of brandy and whisky are required to submit documentary evidence firnished by the place of origin confirming that the products have been aged in wood for a period of at least three years.

— Electronics, electrical and gas consumer products designated as controlled items are required to be registered with the Standards, Productivity and Innovation Board (SPRING Singapore) based on type test report with supporting documents. These products would be required to have a Safety Mark on them or their packaging. Regular and random market surveillance are conducted to ensure that only registered goods with the Safety Mark are supplied in the local market. These products include: components of LPG gas systems, gas cookers, electric cooking ranges, electric irons, microwave ovens, televisions, video cassette recorders, electric fans, electric kettles, immersion water heaters, refrigerators, rice cookers, room air conditioners, vacuum cleaners, washing machines and hi-fi equipment.

— Under the Weights and Measures Regulations, any person in the business of repairing or manufacturing weighing or measuring instruments used for trade

(Continued)

(*Continued*)

Section	Current non-tariff measures applied

must have a valid licence issued by SPRING Singapore. All new or repaired weighing or measuring instruments for trade use must be verified, sealed and stamped by the Weights and Measures Office of SPRING Singapore as prescribed under the Weights and Measures Regulations.

Labeling and Packaging Requirements

— Meat and poultry must have a label containing the description of the product, name and designation number of the slaughterhouse and/or processing establishment, date of slaughtering and/or processing, the batch number, net weight and the country of origin.
— Products with nutritional claim are required to have a nutritional information panel on the label.
— Date-marking is required for perishable and selected 'high-risk' products.
— Labeling requirements exist for paints containing red lead oxide in which the lead content is more than 0.06% by weight or for paints containing other lead components in which the lead content is more than 0.25% by weight.
— Labeling requirements exist for medicines (including Chinese proprietary medicines), poisons and cosmetic products under the relevant legislation.
— Tobacco products are required to display stipulated health warning labels.

Anti-dumping, Countervailing and Safeguard Measures

— Singapore currently does not impose any anti-dumping or countervailing duty.
— Singapore does not have any safeguard legislation.

Excise Duties
Excise duties are charged on four categories of products:

— Motor vehicles (excluding goods vehicles): 12% of Open Market Value (OMV) for motor cycles and scooters; 20% of OMV for other passenger motor vehicles.
— Petroleum products: specific rates

(Continued)

Section	Current non-tariff measures applied
	— Premium petrol (leaded): $7.10/dal — Premium petrol (unleaded): $4.40/dal — Regular petrol (leaded): $6.30/dal — Regular petrol (unleaded): $3.70/dal — Other petrol (leaded): $6.80/dal — Other petrol (unleaded): $4.10/dal — Intoxicating liquors: specific rates, ranging from $0.80/litre–$70/litre of alcohol — Tobacco Products: specific rates, ranging from $151–$293/kg. For cigarettes, the duty imposed will be 29.3 cents for the first gram or part thereof of each stick of cigarette and an additional 29.3 cents for each additional gram or part thereof of each stick of cigarette.
	Singapore charges a flat 5% tax on most goods and services irrespective of whether domestically produced or imported, with the exception of the grant, assignment or surrender of any interest in, or right over, any residential properties, and financial services as listed on the Fourth Schedule to the Goods and Services Tax (GST) Act.

Source: http://www.apec-iap.org

References

Asher, M.G. and R. Sen (2005). "India-East Asia Integration: A Win-Win for Asia", *Economic and Political Weekly*, Vol. XL, No. 36, pp. 3932–3941.

Audretsch, D.B. (2003). "Entrepreneurship, Innovation and Globalization: Does Singapore Need a New Policy Approach?", in Rajan, R.S. (ed.), *Sustaining Competitiveness in the New Global Economy: A Case Study of Singapore*, Cheltenham: Edward Elgar, Chapter 9.

Baldwin, R.E. (2006). "Multilateralising Regionalism: Spaghetti Bowls as Building Blocs on the Path to Global Free Trade", *The World Economy*, 29, pp. 1451–1518.

Bansal, R. (2004). "The Monday Interview: Goh Chok Tong", *Financial Express*, July 12.

Bhaskaran, M. (2003). "Structural Challenges Facing the Singapore Economy", in Rajan, R.S. (ed.), *Sustaining Competitiveness in the New Global Economy: A Case Study of Singapore*, Cheltenham: Edward Elgar, Chapter 7.

Chia, S.Y. (1992). "Foreign Direct Investment in ASEAN Economies", *Asian Development Review*, 5, pp. 60–102.

Das, S.B. and R. Sen (2005). "Singapore-India CECA: Rationale, Overview and Implications", in Pillay, M. (ed.), *Investors Guide to India-Singapore Comprehensive Economic Cooperation Agreement*, Singapore: Reed Elsevier.

FICCI (2005). "FICCII Survey on India Thailand FTA — Emerging Issues", June. Available at http://www.ficci.com/ficci/surveys/The_India_Thailand_FTA-Report.pdf.

Ho, K.W., A.T. Koh and S. Thangavelu (2002). "Enhancing Techno-preneurship: Issues and Challenges", in Koh, A.T., K.L. Lim, W.T. Hui and B. Rao (eds.), *Singapore's Economy in the 21st Century: Issues and Strategies*, Singapore: McGraw Hill.

Hu, A. and J. Shin (2002). "Climbing the Technology Ladder: Challenges Facing Singapore in a Globalized World", in Koh, A.T., K.L. Lim, W.T. Hui and B. Rao (eds.), *Singapore's Economy in the 21st Century: Issues and Strategies*, Singapore: McGraw Hill.

IMF (2000). "Singapore: Selected Issues", *Staff Country Report No. 00/83*, Washington DC: IMF.

Joint Study Group Report (2003). *India-Singapore Comprehensive Economic Cooperation Agreement*, April.

Lee, B.Y. (2002). "Challenges of the New Economy". Available at http://www.mfa.gov.sg/washington/sep2002.pdf.

Lall, S. (2000). "Export Performance, Technological Upgrading and Foreign Direct Investment Strategies in the Asian Newly Industrializing Economies: With Special Reference to Singapore", No. 88, CEPAL, ECLAC. Santiago (October).

Ministry of Trade and Industry, India–Singapore Comprehensive Economic Cooperation Agreement (CECA), *Information Kit*. Available at http://www.fta.gov.sg/.

Rajan, R.S. (2003). "Introduction and Overview: Sustaining Competitiveness in the New Global Economy", in Rajan, R.S. (ed.), *Sustaining Competitiveness in the New Global Economy: A Case Study of Singapore*, Cheltenham: Edward Elgar, Chapter 1.

Rajan, R.S. (2004). "Measures to Attract Foreign Direct Investment: Investment Promotion, Incentives", *Economic and Political Weekly*, 39, January 3, pp. 12–16.

Rajan, R.S. and R. Sen (2002). "Singapore's New Commercial Trade Strategy: The Pros and Cons of Bilateralism", in Chang, L.L. (ed.), *Singapore Perspectives 2002*, Singapore: Times Academic Press, pp. 99–130.

Rajan, R.S. and R. Sen (2005). "The New Wave of Free Trade Agreements in Asia: With Particular Reference to ASEAN, China and India", in *Asian Economic Cooperation and Integration: Progress, Prospects and Challenges*, ADB: Manila.

Rajan, R.S., R. Sen and R. Siregar (2002). "Hong Kong, Singapore and the East Asian Crisis: How Important were Trade Spillovers?" *The World Economy*, 25, pp. 503–537.

Roy, M., J. Marchetti and H. Lim (2006). "Services Liberalization in New Generation of Preferential Trade Agreements: How Much Further than the GATS?", mimeo (September).

Sen, R., M.G. Asher and R.S. Rajan (2004). "ASEAN-India Economic Relations: Current Trends and Future Prospects", *Economic and Political Weekly*, 34, pp. 3297–3309.

Srinath, S. (2005). "Little Credit for Financial Services", *Business Line*, August 3.

Thanadsillapakul, L. (2006). "The Investment Regime in ASEAN Countries", Thailand Law Source, December. Available at http://asialaw.tripod.com/articles/lawaninvestment.html

Thangavelu, S.M. and M.H. Toh (2005). "Bilateral 'WTO-Plus' Free Trade Agreements: The WTO Trade Policy Review of Singapore 2004", *World Economy*, 28, pp. 1211-1228.

Toh, M.H. (2006). "Singapore's Perspectives on the Proliferation of RTAs in East Asia and Beyond", *Global Economic Review*, 35, pp. 259–284.

UNCTAD (2005). "Case study on Outward Foreign Direct Investment by Singaporean Firms: Enterprise Competitiveness and Development", November.

World Bank (2005). *Doing Business in 2005 — Removing Obstacles to Growth*, Washington, DC: Oxford University Press for the World Bank.

World Trade Organisation (WTO) (2004). *Trade Policy Review: Singapore*, WTO. Available at http://www.wto.org/English/tratop_e/tpr_e/tp229_e.htm.

Yeung, H. (2000). "Global Cities and Developmental States: Understanding Singapore's Global Reach", mimeo (March).

Index